D0822556

The First
and the Last

The Comfort of the Triune God in Revelation

Melvin Tinker

If you're looking for 'comfort in trying times,' you may not imagine turning to a mysterious book (Revelation) and an intricate doctrine (the Trinity) to find it. But Melvin Tinker focuses on the clarities rather than the perplexities of Revelation, holding that we are not meant to de-code the book but that the book is given so we can de-code our world. He never allows us to sink into some hermeneutical morass! He zeroes in on the Trinity in Revelation in a way that drives doctrine into life, carries theology into worship (where it belongs), and turns creed toward perseverance. I think chapter 6 (on Revelation 13) should be required reading for all Christians. Let Tinker show you that a throne (the centre that holds) makes all the difference in your world.

Dale Ralph Davis

Retired former Minister in Residence, First Presbyterian Church, South Carolina and Professor of Old Testament at Reformed Theological Seminary, Jackson, Mississippi

Melvin Tinker has a particular knack for writing several books in one— in this case, a commentary on the book of Revelation, a treatise on the doctrine of the Trinity, and a call for Christians to understand our "trying times" and remain faithful to our soon-coming-Lord. Laden with vital biblical truth, rich theological insight, astute cultural acumen and potent historical example, this is a book that will bless both pastors and their people, young and old alike.

Robert S. Smith,

Lecturer in Theology and Ethics, Sydney Missionary & Bible College, Australia

Melvin Tinker ably provides the reader a timely and encouraging meditation on the book of Revelation. This is a terrific engagement with the book of Revelation, conversant with the best of scholarship, and written to help the Christian understand the times in the light of Holy Writ. This is the kind of book we need: deeply immersed in the Scriptures, and brought to bear upon life in the world today."

Brad Green,

Professor of Theological Studies, Union University, Jackson, Tennessee; Professor of Philosophy and Theology, The Southern Baptist Theological Seminary, Louisville, Kentucky; Author, *The Gospel and the Mind*

EP BOOKS

(Evangelical Press) Unit C, Tomlinson Road, Leyland, England, PR25 2DY

www.epbooks.org
epbooks@100fthose.com

© Melvin Tinker 2021. All rights reserved.

First published 2021

British Library Cataloguing in Publication Data

ISBN: 978–1–78397–298–2

Scripture quotations are from The ESV® Bible (The Holy Bible, English Standard Version®), copyright © 2001 by Crossway, a publishing ministry of Good News Publishers. Used by permission. All rights reserved.

Scripture quotations marked NIV in this publication are from the New International Version (NIV), copyright ©1973, 1978, 1984, International Bible Society. Used by permission of Hodder and Stoughton, a member of the Hodder Headline Group. All rights reserved.

For
Philip, Vicki, Rosie and Lydia

With love and admiration

Contents

Introduction

INCREASINGLY WITHIN CHURCH CIRCLES THERE ARE TWO common reactions to two words. The first word is 'theology'. This tends to produce a big yawn — what has theology got to do with anything contemporary? In the day of the immediate, the impressive and the inspirational, theology simply seems out of place. It is often associated with the distant, the dry and the dull. Certainly, there may be some who get a buzz out of debating the attributes of God and all those 'omni' words — omnipotence, omniscience and omnipresence, but what have these to do with my struggle with cancer, the threatening nature of climate change and issue of mass migration? In a desperate attempt to be relevant and engage with these kinds of questions, some church ministers have been tempted to replace, or at last supplement, the Bible with other things — mindfulness, 'Gaia theory' and the environment, or various political ideologies.

It has not always been the case. Once the minister was viewed as a 'physician of the soul' and the Bible as the most practical book on earth, like a doctor's black bag, with medicine to meet the requirements of needy people.

This was especially so with that often maligned group of Christians known as the Puritans. One of their number, William Ames, described theology in very practical terms, as 'the doctrine of living unto God'.[1] Theology was for living, enabling God's people to live in God's world, God's way. This meant that it was vital to see the world as God sees it, as it really is, cutting through all the falsehoods and fabrications which would construe things differently in a man-centred way.

Similarly, the great 'Sweet Dropper', Richard Sibbes of Cambridge, depicted the church as a common hospital, such that theology in his hands was 'essentially Christ shaped comfort for a weary, needy, broken people'.[2] Is there anything more relevant to a sick person than having access to a treatment which can cure them? Likewise, there is nothing more relevant to a sick world and hurting, bewildered Christians, than theology. The source of theology is the whole of the Bible, which, as J.I. Packer reminds us, is a 'doctrinal book'.[3] This is where we find truth about ourselves, the world and God which is vital for genuine human flourishing, 'whereas fallen man sees himself as the centre of the universe, the Bible shows us God as central, and depicts all creatures, man included, in their proper perspective — as existing through God and for God.'[4]

The second word is apocalypse. The reaction to this is often one of bewilderment. In common parlance it has become a metaphor for some impending end of the world scenario, a doomsday. Even when it is rightly understood as a term which describes a literary genre and more specifically the last book in the Bible, the Book of Revelation, this only adds to people's sense of angst. When Christians turn to it, it is so unlike anything else in the New Testament (with the exception of Jesus' teaching in Mark 13 and parallels). It appears to be more of a dream than a progressive story.[5] Knowing that it has been a treasure trove which has been plundered for all sorts of 'end of time' teaching ranging from the cautious to the audacious, the believer may well be tempted to give it a miss and retreat to more familiar territory like 1 Peter. That would be a mistake.

It really is the case that, 'The Book of Revelation is the most remarkable text you will ever read.'[6] It is also the most comforting and challenging. Once we have mastered some basic principles of interpretation, overcoming our understandable 'imageophobia' (I have just made up that word!), the Book of the Apocalypse in its own distinctive way does all those things which the rest of the Bible does, showing that God is central to everything. We are to joyfully embrace that perspective.

If, in the words of Ames, theology is the 'doctrine of living unto God', the Book of Revelation is theology par excellence. In his own distinctive way, John serves up for God's tested and tempted people a vision of Reality which is second to none, firing our imagination as well as strengthening our faith. John can rightly be said to be a minister of reality, witnessing in a remarkable way to what is in Christ — hidden from the world but revealed to the church.7 'The main purpose of the book of Revelation,' according to William Hendriksen, 'is to comfort the militant Church in its struggle against evil.'8 It mainly does this by drawing our hearts to the one true God who is Father, Son and Holy Spirit.

As we shall see, the doctrine of the Trinity in the Apocalypse is not only the most highly developed in the whole of the Bible, it brackets human history, undergirds reality and provides the bedrock for Christian hope. The God who is the 'Alpha and Omega', the Lamb who is the 'First and the Last' and the sevenfold Spirit who mediates God's revelation and presence to his people, provides all that is necessary to ensure that whatever Christians might have to endure in the world, they, like their Saviour, are victorious (3:21; 19:14). Here is a vision of God, transcendent and yet near, almighty and yet tender, ruling and rescuing. This is the God of the Christian faith.

What follows is a series of expositions which tease out the theological and pastoral aspects of the Book of Revelation. This involves setting the passages in their original context in order to enable us to engage with the contemporary scene of Christians living in the West. We shall discover that many of the pressures the first Christians faced are very similar to the ones we are facing today. What is more, the comfort John's visions provide for his first readers come home to us with an amazing immediacy. John's world, the world of the Apocalypse, is very much our world and his God our God, in all his triune majesty.

I would like to thank Mark Lanier for the use of his remarkable library in Houston, which enabled me to dig deeper into the background of the Apocalypse. Thanks also to Shirley Godbold and Philip Tinker for checking the manuscript and making all the necessary corrections. Last, but not least, there is my heartfelt gratitude to my wife Heather, for her constant encouragement and support.

Soli Deo Gloria

Melvin Tinker
The Lanier Theological Library

1. Getting Real: the Trinity and the Apocalypse

Christians are always more culturally short-sighted than they realise. They are often unable to tell, for instance, where their Christian principles leave off and their cultural perspectives begin. Many fail to ask themselves the important question: 'Where are we coming from and what is our own context?'[1]

So writes the Christian social critic, Os Guinness. This is nothing new. It was a problem faced by the early Christians. Indeed, it was a pressing issue directly addressed by the risen and ascended Jesus Christ in the letter to the seven churches in Asia Minor as found in the first three chapters of the Book of Revelation.

Let's take one example of a church which was selling out to the surrounding culture rather than standing out from it: the church at Laodicea.

And to the angel of the church in Laodicea write: 'The words of the Amen, the faithful and true witness, the beginning of God's creation. I know your works: you are neither cold nor hot. Would that you were either cold or hot! So, because you are lukewarm, and neither hot nor cold, I will spit you out of my mouth. For you say, I am rich, I have prospered, and I need nothing, not realizing that you are wretched, pitiable, poor, blind, and naked. I counsel you to buy from me gold refined by fire, so that you may be rich, and white garments so that you may clothe yourself and the shame of your nakedness may not be seen, and salve to anoint your eyes, so that you may see. Those whom I love, I reprove and discipline, so be zealous and repent. Behold, I stand at the door and knock. If anyone hears my voice and opens the door, I will come in to him and eat with him, and he with me. The one who conquers, I will grant him to sit with me on my throne, as I also conquered and sat down with my Father on his throne. He who has an ear, let him hear what the Spirit says to the churches.' (3:14–22)

This is a church which, to put it bluntly, had become useless. The key to understanding the nature of Jesus rebuke lies in the imagery being used associated with the plumbing system of this ancient city. In the Lycus valley where Laodicea was situated, there were two other New Testament towns, Colossae and Hierapolis. Colossae enjoyed water which was fresh and cold and therefore useful as drinking water. Hierapolis, on the other hand, had water which was warm and medicinal; it was a spa town, having hot springs in which people bathed to improve their health. Its water was also useful. Laodicea, however, had to draw its water from a long distance by stone pipes. This left thick carbonate deposits in the pipes and not surprisingly Laodicean water had become proverbial for its obnoxious taste. In effect, the Lord Jesus was saying to this church: 'I wish that you were like the water of Colossae — cold and useful. Or like the water of Hierapolis — hot and useful, but you are neither. You have become like the water your citizens drink — lukewarm, indigestible and so useless, indeed worse than useless; think of how your stomach retches when you sip that disgusting mix piped into your town. That is how I feel when I look at the way you are conducting yourselves. You make me want to throw up.' That is the unsanitised version of 3:16![2]

What was it about these Christians which provoked such a violent reaction from the risen and ascended Lord? Had they denied the faith? Not openly. Had they sold out to sexual licence like the church in Thyatira? Not really. We see those things mentioned in some of the other letters, but not in this instance. What, then, was their problem? We are told in 3:17, 'For you say, I am rich, I have prospered, and I need nothing, not realizing that you are wretched, pitiable, poor, blind, and naked.' The church had simply begun to mirror the city of which it was a part. Instead of countering the surrounding culture and so transforming it, it had surrendered to the culture and had therefore been captured by it. Put simply, the church had become worldly.

When the world is in the church rather than the church in the world

Worldliness is not to be understood in a crass reductionistic way, such that if only Christians refrain from smoking, drinking, gambling etc. they will be unworldly. It is possible to forego such things and yet still be worldly in the sense that the prevailing values and outlook of the culture in which a church finds itself are taken on board by Christians without any critical assessment, thus forming an unholy alliance. For those living in Laodicea towards the end of the first century, it was a matter of adopting the outlook of Rome, that wealth, power and prestige were what ultimately mattered and defined a person (which is not that far removed from the outlook of our society). Who you were was linked to what you were and what you had.[3] By the standards of the surrounding society, the Christians in Laodicea had it all, so they thought, until the Lord Jesus disabused them of their delusion by employing these devastating metaphors. They had a friendship with the world, which amounted to enmity with God (James 4:4; cf. 1 John 2:15).

Christians in the West today are subject to similar shaping forces, in particular the corrosive effects of secularisation. This is defined by Bryan Wilson as 'the process whereby religious thinking, practice and institutions lose their social significance'.[4] One effect of this process is what Max Weber calls rationalisation. This relates to religious ideas becoming less and less meaningful and religious traditions becoming more marginal as they are replaced by other modes of thinking and traditions. With the advance of modernity less space is reserved for God. It is taken as a 'given' that if you are ill you call a physician not a priest; if you want good crops you get a better fertiliser, you don't offer sacrifices to appease an angry deity. This is the hallmark of modernity, a 'bottom up' causation of human designs and products to replace the 'top down' causation of God and the supernatural.[5] This in turn gives rise to the modernist mentality summarised by the social scientist, Philip Rieff: 'What characterises modernity, I think, is just this idea that men need not submit to any power — higher or lower — other than their own.'[6]

The way this worldly mentality has made inroads into the modern church is evidenced by the Church Growth Movement. It has been argued that certain expressions of this movement exhibit a new form of worldliness which results from being squeezed into a practical secular mould by secularisation. Here we have an ecclesiastical manifestation of the 'bottom up' causation of human designs and products, spoken of by Guinness.[7] 'The emphasis on the quantifiable and the "doable" [what can be achieved] is, of course, a key feature of secularisation. In this movement we have both in bucket loads, especially in the United States. Having encountered this, a visiting Japanese businessman commented to an Australian, "Whenever I meet a Buddhist leader, I meet a holy man. Whenever I meet a Christian leader, I meet a manager."'[8] Bearing in mind Rieff's chief characteristic of modernity ('men not wanting to submit to any power — higher or lower — than their own'), the following citation from a church growth manual frighteningly sums up the modern mentality:

> The church is a business. Marketing is essential for a business to operate successfully. The Bible is one of the world's great marketing texts. However, the point is indisputable: the Bible does not warn against the evils of marketing. So it behoves us not to spend time bickering about techniques and processes. Think of your church not as a religious meeting place, but as a service agency — an entity that exists to satisfy people's needs. The marketing plan is the Bible of the marketing game; everything that happens in the life of the product occurs because the plan wills it. It is critical that we keep in mind the fundamental principle of Christian communication: the audience, not the message, is sovereign.[9]

The result, as David Wells argues, is that truth shrinks and the church eventually disappears:

> There is a yearning in the evangelical world today. We encounter it everywhere. It is a yearning for what is real. Sales pitches, marketed faith, the gospel as commodity, people as customers, God as just a prop to my inner life, the glitz and sizzle. Disneyland on the loose in our churches — all of it skin deep and often downright wrong. It is not making serious disciples. It cannot make serious disciples. It brims with success, but it is empty, shallow, and indeed unpardonable.[10]

The irony is that the soul destroying effect which secularisation has on society in general is taking its toll on the church in particular. This is all very Laodicean.

What goes around comes around

You may be thinking: What has this to do with the Book of Revelation? The answer is: everything! How we imagine the world to be will inevitably shape how we think and act.[11] Secularisation has effectively squeezed God out of most people's thinking. Accordingly faith is restricted to the private world and is not allowed to intrude into the public square. That is the propaganda of our age — politicians in the UK 'don't do God' to quote former adviser to Tony Blair, Alastair Campbell.

The early Christians were engaged in a different culture war to our own, namely, that it was Cæsar and not Christ who was Lord. This was not secularisation but 'Cæsarisation'. This lay at the heart of the imperial cult: 'Awe and gratitude are two emotional responses that local representations of imperial cult ceremony, presence, and propaganda sought to arouse towards Rome and its emperors among the local populace.'[12] Some of the churches in Asia Minor had, in different ways and in varying degrees, capitulated to this. They had adopted a 'fake reality', which was nothing short of idolatrous.

The way in which this is countered by God through his servant John, is not simply by way of commands and encouragements (although they are there; 'Whoever has ears, let them hear'), but mainly by presenting a different way of viewing things, an alternate higher reality, a true picture of the way things actually are:

> On earth the powers of evil challenge God's role and even masquerade as the ultimate power over all things, claiming divinity. But heaven is the sphere of ultimate reality: what is true in heaven must become true on earth. Thus John is taken up into heaven to see that God's throne is the ultimate reality behind all earthly appearances. Having seen God's sovereignty in heaven, he can then see how it must come to be acknowledged on earth.[13]

Applied to our context, the secularised world is a 'world without windows', to use a phrase popularised by Peter Berger, where people no longer see the world as a gift (a created order), but a given (a wholly natural order).[14] The Book of the Apocalypse exposes such thinking for what it is: a lie.

Imagine there's a heaven

More recently, the way in which we perceive life and so act accordingly has been explored by Charles Taylor. He speaks of the 'social imaginary'.[15] This is the 'picture' that frames everyday beliefs and practices, in particular the 'ways people imagine their social existence'.[16] Kevin Vanhoozer describes it as:

> … that nest of background assumptions, often implicit, that lead people to feel things as right or wrong, correct or incorrect. It is another name for the root metaphor

(or root narrative) that shapes a person's perception of the world, undergirds one's worldview, and funds one's plausibility structure ... A social imaginary is not a theory — the creation of intellectuals — but a storied way of thinking. It is the taken-for-granted story of the world assumed and passed on by a society's characteristic language, pictures, and practices. A social imaginary is not taught in universities but by cultures, insofar as it is "carried in images, stories and legends." People become secular not by taking classes in Secularity 101 but simply by participating in a society that no longer refers to God the way it used to. "God" makes only rare appearances in contemporary literature, art, and television ... Social imaginaries ... are the metaphors and stories by which we live, the images and narratives that indirectly indoctrinate us.[17]

What the Book of Revelation presents is a different 'social imaginary' — not a fiction, but a higher reality to help us envisage our situation properly. The book itself is, if you will, an opening of the windows of the universe, as well as being a cosmic map, using symbols and signs (like maps do) to lay out a model of reality to enable Christians to 'get real'. The book enables them to align their lives as individuals and as congregations with this reality which has the triune God at the centre of it all: 'The worship scenes of Revelation 4 and 5 articulate a model of a well-ordered cosmos in which all created beings in every region of the map turn towards this one centre — the throne of God and the Lamb — to offer grateful adoration.'[18] This is how Clifford Geertz describes what is happening with the Book of Revelation as a form of divine communication, that:

> … alters, often radically, the whole landscape presented to common sense, alters it in such a way that the moods and motivations induced by religious practice seem themselves practical, the only sensible ones to adopt given the way things 'really' are.[19]

The world of the secularised person (which includes the 'secularised' Christian) is way too small and far too man-centred. People scornfully tell Christians to 'get real' and to live in 'the real world' by which they mean, of course, a world without God, without wider horizons, without doors into heaven. But the Bible makes it clear that we will never understand our world unless we understand this world: the heavenly world, which is just as real as the earthly one. Invisibility is not to be confused with unreality. God has given us this revelation of John not so that we might escape from this world, and certainly not that we might conform to it, but so that we may live in it as we should, seeing its passing-away pretensions and power politics in their true light. Robert Mounce is correct in his assessment that, 'A true insight into history is gained only when we view all things from the vantage point of the heavenly throne.'[20]

This is one of the main reasons for teaching doctrine in the church. Doctrine is designed to enable Christians to think properly and imagine rightly, to have their minds 'transformed' rather than being 'conformed' to the world (Romans 12:1). The Book of Revelation is especially well positioned to capture the imagination by its very nature with its symbols, metaphors and high drama. The Roman imperial cult employed such symbols and drama too in order to capture the hearts and minds of its citizens, but what we see in the Apocalypse outshines them all, showing them up to be a pale, blasphemous imitation of the real thing, as will become clear when we turn to Revelation 13.

A totally different perspective is given to the churches by John. 'He confronts them with a well-developed picture of how their society's practices and ideologies "look" sub specie aeternitatis, in the light of eternity from the perspective of that "longer view" that reaches before and after the story of the Roman imperialism.'[21] There is nothing more practical if you are on a difficult journey than having an accurate map. The Book of Revelation is therefore eminently practical for Christians and churches as they make their way through this world to the next.

Being literary without being literal

Some within the church might be content with simple propositions and commands such as, 'God is in charge and we are to be different.' That might penetrate a bit below the surface of our minds but will do little to get us to see things differently and motivate us to act earnestly, especially when faced with opposition. We must come to terms with what Christians and most people experience on a moment by moment basis from a world which has decided to exclude God from his universe. Through pictures, stories, education, entertainment, 'infotainment' and lives lived out around us, we are continuingly being presented with a very different 'social imaginary' to that of the Bible. There are also the additional social pressures to conform, or else become the target of Twitter frenzy![22] The Christian needs more than straightforward statements and commands if he is not only to resist these shaping influences but to counter them. God in his wisdom knows this, hence speaking to his people through this type of literature called apocalyptic, meaning literally, a 'lifting the veil'. This not only informs the mind but stirs the imagination and the heart as well.

But how do we read this book responsibly, paying attention to its intended meaning? Ian Paul gives a helpful illustration:

> 'The stars will fall from heaven;
> the sun will cease its shining;
> The moon will be turned to blood,
> and fire and hail will fall from heaven.
> The rest of the country will have
> sunny intervals with scattered showers.'

Reading this usually brings a smile to one's face — but why? The language is in many ways similar; the vocabulary in all three lines describes cosmological phenomena; and there is even a shared two-part structure to each line. The answer is, of course, that we instantly recognise the first two lines as a different genre, or kind of writing, from the third line. This is not something we will probably have been taught … most of us learn to recognise different kinds of writing simply by experience, by seeing different examples and noticing what they have in common.[23]

He then goes on to give two reasons why it is vital to recognise genre. First, 'genre is shaped by the relationship between the author and the anticipated audience for what is written.' We ourselves adopt different styles depending upon who it is we are addressing and what it is we are communicating. For example, we use an informal style in a letter to a friend, and a more structured approach if writing a technical manual.

Secondly, 'genre tells us how to interpret what has been written.' A piece of writing which begins, 'Once upon a time' will be interpreted quite differently from one which starts, 'The weather forecast for tomorrow is …' The question for us, is where are we to place the Book of Revelation in terms of genre? The opening chapter gives several indications.

First, it is a 'revelation' (1:1), 'The revelation of Jesus Christ'. This is the word '*apokalypsis*' from which we get our word 'apocalypse'. It doesn't mean the catastrophic end of the world; it literally means 'pulling aside the veil' in order to allow us to glimpse something which otherwise would remain hidden. Here we are told that Jesus is the one who both pulls the curtain aside and is the content of what is being revealed.[24] This is a revelation which comes from God, who gives it to Jesus, who sent his angel to John, who writes to God's people.

Secondly, it is a 'prophecy' (1:3), 'Blessed is the one

who reads aloud the words of this prophecy.' We tend to associate prophecy with predicting the future. While there may be some prediction occurring here, that is not the main purpose of prophecy. A better way of describing biblical prophecy would be 'the proclamation of God's plan'. Seeing prophecy solely as prediction can lead us astray into thinking that whatever is, will be — a kind of fatalism — whereas much prophecy, including the prophecy of the Book of Revelation, is conditional. If people continue down a certain path, some things are going to happen as a result (which could be good or bad) but if they change direction, what will happen will also change. We may think of it like this: if I am on the corner of a street and I see you stepping out into the road at the same moment a bus is coming towards you unseen, and I shout 'Watch out!', in a way I am being a prophet. I am looking into the future (which may be seconds away from what is going to happen) and proclaim something to you in order for you to do something about it. Much of what we find in the Book of Revelation is a call for people, especially Christians, to change direction before it is too late. Of course, what John presents is much more than that. He writes as a Christian prophet who announces the imminent fulfilment of earlier biblical prophecies (10:7; 22:10).[25]

Thirdly, it is a 'letter', and like many other letters in the New Testament, there is a named sender and recipient (1:4), 'John, to the seven churches that are in Asia.' The correspondent is someone called 'John', traditionally identified with John the son of Zebedee. Some argue for a different 'John', such as the so called 'John the Elder'. In terms of his own identification, he says he is a brother and fellow sufferer for the kingdom (1:9). He is located on the island of Patmos, a small island lying about thirty-seven miles south-west of Asia Minor. The reason for him being there is 'on account of the word of God and the testimony of Jesus'. The Christian historian, Eusebius, understood this in the light of the tradition that John was exiled to Patmos during the reign of Domitian as a result of his activity in the churches.[26] What really matters is that we recognise the ultimate author of this letter, the risen and ascended Lord Jesus.

Who is addressed? We are told: 'the seven churches in that are in Asia'. These churches existed in part of the western area of what we know as Turkey, and the churches are specifically named in 1:11. Although these churches were the primary recipients as they are addressed directly, the fact that seven churches are chosen may also suggest a wider audience in that the 'seven' are in some ways representative of the whole of God's people.[27]

In terms of the genre, then, the book is a mix of epistle, prophecy and apocalyptic. The latter uses symbols, colours and numbers which have significance for the readers, much of which, as we shall see, is drawn from the Old Testament. In fact it is the Old Testament theology of God as the one true God who is creator and redeemer which is dominant throughout. This God alone is worthy of worship, trust and gratitude.

In terms of historical and cultural location the imagery

which is to the fore is that of imperial submission. The wearing of white, bowing down, the casting of crowns, the cry 'worthy', on the human level are twisted into idolatrous expressions of gratitude and trust to the 'saviour rulers' who bring 'peace' (the Pax Romana) but it is all fake. These expressions of devotion belong to God alone as we see especially in chapters 4 and 5.

> Jesus' words to Pilate, "You have no power except what has been given to you from above" (John 19:11, NIV), are refracted through this visionary lens, spoken to all human power. Power that demands allegiance over against or ahead of the God and Father of the Lord Jesus Christ is speaking a lie and based on deceit; if we are tempted to believe it, we need our eyes opened to the true source of all things. God alone is worthy of our unceasing praise, our unswerving loyalty and our profound gratitude."[28]

Ultimate reality

Over and against the pretensions to power and glory of earthly rulers, who as they present themselves are without doubt impressive and intimidating, the Book of Revelation encourages God's people, and anyone who has 'ears to hear', to take with the utmost seriousness the overwhelming reality of God. Not God as humans imagine him (another expression of our idolatrous hearts), but as he reveals himself to be. The God who occupies the throne of heaven, the place of supreme order and beauty is triune. As we shall see, the self-revelation of God is completely at one with the monotheism of the Old Testament, for example the classic '*Shema*' of Deuteronomy 6:4: 'Hear, O Israel: The LORD our God, the LORD is one.' Not two or three or twenty-six, but one. However, even here the word translated 'one' is '*echad*' (dx'a) which allows for some sort of complexity or plurality within that oneness. The same word (*echad*) is used of husband and wife becoming 'one' flesh in Genesis 2:24 through the act of sexual union, or the gathering of the tribes of Israel together as 'one' man in Judges 20:1. So an over-translation of this verse would be: 'Hear, O Israel: The LORD our God, the LORD is oneness.'[29] The God we meet in the first chapter of the book is not a singular god or a lonely god, but one who within his own eternal perfect Being self-exists as three persons, Father, Son and Holy Spirit. It is this God in his triune majesty enthroned at the centre of the universe who is its source and goal. He is the ultimate reality from which all other realities derive their being, significance and value. Not to worship this God is to be guilty of idolatry, as all we are left with is, in the words of John Calvin, the 'bare and empty name of God' not the reality.[30]

God in three persons

If we are to understand the world properly as both created and fallen, and the place and future of the church in God's great plan of redemption, we need to have some measure of understanding of the Trinity:

> The Trinity is, then, a very important Christian doctrine

to put into practice. Without it, our faith is far less distinct from any other religion. With it, we see the deepest realities of what it means to be a Christian … The doctrine of the Trinity describes the name of our God — a God unlike any of the other 'pretenders' to the title. It also gives direction to our prayers, reminding us that we only come before the Father through sharing in the sonship of the Son and receiving his Spirit. It teaches us to approach God in humility, as adopted children who are 'at table' with him purely by his grace … The doctrine of the Trinity also teaches us the true meaning of love, because it shows us the sacrificial nature of God at work.'[31]

The Apocalypse introduces us to the triune God in a distinctive and awe-inspiring way. Let us read on and worship.

2. The Triune God of Revelation

Soon after the outbreak of World War II, the Prime Minister, Winston Churchill, gave a broadcast to the nation in which he described Russia as 'a riddle wrapped in a mystery, inside an enigma'. In other words, this was a nation which was *very* difficult to understand, and, of course, it still is! Its thinking and its ways seem impenetrable to most people living in the West. Some would argue that what could be said of Russia could also be said of Revelation, the Book of the Apocalypse. The basic problem is that we are not used to reading anything like this. However, that wasn't the experience of the first Christians because there were other similar writings, full of the same kind of dream-like imagery, evocative symbols, garish colours and numbers filled with significance.[1] What may seem obscure to *us* in our location in history was far from obscure to the first readers, not least because much of what we find here comes from the Old Testament. As Peter Leithart says, 'John writes *with* Scripture rather than *about* it. John paints an apocalypse, and the OT is his palette.'[2] That's about right. In reading this powerful book you soon discover it to be grounded in the world of the Old Testament, but with a specific application to the world in which we all live.

The pastoral purpose

As we saw in the first chapter, this is a letter/prophecy written with certain situations and needs in mind. While there is the addressing of actual first century congregations in Asia Minor, the problems they faced are problems which Christians throughout the world and throughout the ages constantly face, especially the temptation to fall out of the Christian race. On the one hand believers need to be confronted when yielding to the pressure to give way and give up. They also need to be positively spurred on to 'keep keeping on'. Brian Tabb summarises the main thrust of the book well:

> Revelation's symbolic visions *challenge* readers to resist worldly compromise, spiritual complacency and false teaching. They also *encourage* embattled believers to persevere in faithful witness and hope in the present and future reign of God and the Lamb. The visions offer a divine perspective on what is true, valuable and lasting. They expose the true nature of the world's political, cultural, economic and religious system

destined for destruction, and they orient believers' world views and values around God's eternal kingdom.[3]

Those facing hard times need to be encouraged to persevere. We see that in the first three chapters, where the risen and ascended Christ talks about those who are victorious (*nikon* in Greek e.g. 2:10) with a promise of a future blessing as a reward for their faithfulness. But this is not just a matter of weathering the political and heretical storms in stoic fashion, for the importance of positively witnessing (Greek *marturia*) to Christ is stressed time and time again (1:2, 9; 3:14; 2:13; 11:3–13). John wants conquerors, those who do not withdraw from the world but engage with it through prophetic witness. In line with this, de Silva writes:

> John orients the disciples toward their situation as a set of challenges to overcome, and in the light of the "larger picture," a set of forces to be overcome, not least through resistance unto the end. The identity that John asks the disciples to embrace and enact is *O Nikon* (the victor), the one who persists in overcoming.[4]

In such situations there is always the temptation to compromise and so prove faithless. This begins to happen when we start seeing the world and its God-opposed ways as something we have to come to terms with, to deal with by keeping our heads down and mouths shut, to hold belief in private, but not cause any waves by standing out in public. We see such a concern in the letters to the seven churches where some believers have decided to take this easy option of 'going with the flow' with the result that they are almost indistinguishable from the pagans around them. Because of this the risen Christ called them to repent (especially Thyatira and Sardis).

The question is: how are Christians to be comforted and challenged in order to ensure that how they behave remains in line with what they believe?

Reality check

The answer is by getting to grips with reality, the way things *really are* and not be seduced by the way things *appear* to be. In other words, there is a need to be exposed to the *truth* of God and his plans and purposes for the world.

As we saw with Charles Taylor's idea of the 'social imaginary', what we imagine to be the case will invariably effect how we go about living. Just think about it. The controlling narrative of our society is that the world has come from nowhere and is heading nowhere, and this leads people to start thinking and acting as if people are nobodies. Life then becomes cheap, hence easy access to abortions and calls for euthanasia. The pursuit of pleasure becomes all-consuming, because where else are we going to gain satisfaction during our short stay on this planet? When this is repeated day-in and day-out by the media, educationalists, the entertainment industry and so on, Christians will, unless they are very careful, start to adopt some of these views for themselves or at least adapt their beliefs to fit in with them.

But if reality is more than what we can see and touch, having an invisible spiritual dimension (a God who made us and who is personally active in his world, as well as a devil who opposes him operating through political and culture shaping structures to deceive us), then we need to know that so we can act accordingly. That is, we need a map which is an accurate representation of the way things are, so we can negotiate our way through life. The world is giving us faulty maps which result in people being hurt and getting lost. God gives us an accurate map so we can thrive as God intended.

This is where the Book of Revelation provides us with a map of ultimate reality: 'the book's symbolic visions shapes believers' world views around what is true, good and beautiful according to God's revealed standards and motivates them to live counter-culturally in the world as a follower of the Lamb wherever he goes.'⁵ The Book of Revelation isn't a riddle, wrapped in a mystery which requires some kind of code to understand. Rather, it is the final book in the Bible which is meant to help us decode the world so we can understand it, and figure out what is really going on behind all the fake news, the pressures of political correctness, and the attempts to shape our thoughts by distorting the truth, but with the reassurance that no matter what happens God is still God and will be victorious!

However, this raises certain fundamental questions: who is this God who will be the victor? Is he powerful enough to win, or might the devil outmanoeuvre and beat him? Does he care enough to ensure he wins or might he be fickle and change his mind and decide to give up on us? Is he a God who is bound by time as we are, and so might grow old and get tired? Everything turns on the nature and character of God. And just what that nature and character is, is intended to drive us to our knees in worship and out into the world in witness. What we need to know is given to us in the opening verses of the book:

> Grace to you and peace from him who is and who was and who is to come, and from the seven spirits who are before his throne, and from Jesus Christ the faithful witness, the firstborn of the dead, and the ruler of kings on earth. (1:4–5)

A close encounter of the divine kind

Straight away we are introduced to God as he really is and not as we imagine him to be. We encounter the one true God, who exists within his own being in a joyful fellowship of love between Father, Son and Holy Spirit. In some ways the whole Book of Revelation is about delighting in the Trinity. As Ian Paul claims, the Book of Revelation has 'the most developed trinitarian theology of any New Testament book'.[6]

You might want to ask: how do we get the Trinity from these verses? The answer is not all that difficult. First of all, John writes that 'grace and peace' come to these Christians scattered around Asia Minor (modern-day Turkey). In some ways this reflects the standard Christian adaptation of the traditional Greek 'greetings' (*charein*) and Jewish blessing 'peace' (*shalom*), which Paul normally extends from 'God the Father and the Lord Jesus Christ' (e.g. Romans 1:7). But in the opening to this book there is a significant elaboration because of the distinctive titles of the triune God which 'prepares readers for the absolute centrality of God in the symbolic universe of the Apocalypse'.[7]

Grace is the undeserved kindness of God to sinners and peace flows from it as its fruit: peace with God, peace in our hearts, and peace with each other (cf. Ephesians 2:17; John 14:27). In the Bible the great blessings of grace and peace have one source — God. And yet here John says there are *three* sources: 'Grace and peace to you *from* [here is the first one] him who is, and who was and who is to come, *and from* [here is the second] the seven spirits ... *and* [the third] from Jesus Christ.' If God is the source of grace and peace, and there is only *one* God, yet *three* sources are mentioned here, this suggests that there are three persons within the being of God, sharing the divine nature, because they are all equal sources of the divine blessings of grace and peace.

Let's take each person of the Trinity in turn and ask: who is he and what does he do?

God the Father

First, John speaks of the Father in his eternity and unchangeableness, the one 'who is, and who was and who is to come', sovereignly present at every point in history, not only the history of the world but the history of every person living in it. This is repeated and unpacked a little further in 1:8. '"I am the Alpha and the Omega," says the Lord God, *"who is and who was and who is to come,* the Almighty."' It is highly unlikely that we would have written it that way. We would naturally have spoken of God as the one who *was,* is and is to come, putting the past tense first. But it is the present tense John uses. Why?[8]

Here is an instance of Revelation drawing on the Old Testament, taking us to Exodus chapter 3. Here Moses encounters God in the burning bush and asks what should he tell Israel about the name of their God, and God replies, 'I AM WHO I AM' (3:14). This is the God whose very *name* — 'I AM' (YHWH) — means commitment, a declaration that, 'All that I am, I am for *you*. All that I will ever need *to be*, will be for you.' (The covenantal significance in this name is suggested in Exodus 3:12, 'I will *be* with you' which precedes Moses, question of God's identity.) Even when John portrays the immensity and majesty of God, he does so in a way that reassures his people that this God is at their side. He will lead them as he led Israel, through this wilderness of a world gone wrong, into his Promised Land of heaven. To be sure God has no origin, he just *is* 'I AM' which was translated as *Yahweh*. That is a personal name, but there is security in that name for God's people because of his unchangeableness. It means he doesn't tire out or change his mind, being one thing one day and different another day, God the Father is totally dedicated to the salvation of his people whatever happens, and will never change.

This is what theologians refer to as the *aseity* of God (from the Latin *a se* meaning 'from himself'). This is no needy God, requiring a creation because he is lonely. Consequently he is not dependent upon his creation for anything. This is the 'life in himself' of which Jesus speaks in John 5:26. The great medieval theologian Anselm speaks of it in these terms, that God, 'has of himself all that he has, while other things have nothing of themselves. And other things having nothing of themselves, have their only reality from him.'9 This understanding, that creation is contingent on God, is reflected in the great hymn of praise in 4:11, 'Worthy are you, our Lord and God, to receive glory and honour and power, for you created all things, and by your will they existed and were created.' These truths are fleshed out by the other titles of God which surround it in 1:8.

He is the 'Alpha and Omega'. Alpha is the letter which stands at the beginning of the Greek alphabet and Omega the final letter, marking its end. This tells us something about God's *eternal relation to the world.* He precedes all things, originates all things and is steering all things to their ultimate goal which, as we shall see as the book unfolds, is the bringing of everything together under Christ's Lordship. 'God precedes all things, as their Creator, and he will bring all things to eschatological fulfilment. He is the origin and goal of all history. He has the first word, in creation, and the last word, in new creation.'10

The entire universe comes from God, belongs to God

and is being ruled by God. It is not possible even to begin to compare anything with this God; he brackets the universe like alpha and omega bracket the alphabet. What is more, he brackets your life and mine. He was there when you were being formed in your mother's womb (Psalm 139); he was there when you were growing up; he was there when you became a Christian believer and will be there when you are ready to leave this world for the next; he is *our* alpha and omega.

He is also the 'Lord God *Almighty*' (Greek *ho pantokrator*). Seven times the Apocalypse uses the full phrase, 'the Lord God Almighty' (seven is the number of perfection or fullness). The term 'Almighty' doesn't refer to abstract power, meaning 'God has more muscle than anyone else.' Rather, it concerns God's *executive power*, using that power to control everything for the sake of his people and the glory of his name. This is why Paul can say that, 'for those who love God all things work together for good,' (Romans 8:28); that is what this tender executive power of God the Father does.

God the Son

> ... *and from Jesus Christ* the faithful witness, the firstborn of the dead, and the ruler of kings on earth. (1:5)

John is setting the stage for Revelation's kaleidoscopic portrait of the Lord Jesus, the supreme sovereign who saves his people by his own blood shed on a cross and returns to execute divine judgement on his foes, 1:7.

'Behold, he is coming with the clouds, and every eye will
see him, even those who pierced him, and all tribes of the
earth will wail on account of him' (1:7).[11]

It should not be overlooked that the titles given to God
the Father are also given to Jesus the Son. In 1:8 *God*
says, 'I am the Alpha and the Omega.' In 1:17, *Christ*
says, 'I am the first and the last.' In fact this is *Yahweh's*
self-designation as we find it for example in Isaiah 44:6
and 48:12, two of the great monotheistic passages in
the Old Testament: 'I am the first and I am the last;
besides me there is no god'; 'I am he; I am the first,
and I am the last.' Yahweh was sometimes vocalised as
Yahoh and transliterated into Greek (the language of the
New Testament) as IAO (Iota, Alpha, Omega). What is
said of God is being said of Jesus Christ without any
hint of apology or sign of embarrassment. Given the
absolute commitment to monotheism the Jews had, this
is extraordinary (and is reaffirmed at the end of the book
in 22:12–13, 'Behold I am coming soon … I am the Alpha
and the Omega, the first and the last, the beginning and
the end.)'

As the alpha, the beginning, he is the one through
whom the universe came into being in all its awesome
vastness, its mind numbing complexity and breathtaking
beauty. As the omega, the end, he is the one who moment
by moment enables every single atom to spin in the far
flung worlds on the outer reaches of the galaxies, and
providentially directs every event in this world for the sake
of the people he came to save.[12]

The equation is clear. What is true of the Father regarding his deity is true of the Son. Put simply, Jesus *is* God. However, 1:8 which affirms Jesus' divinity needs to be qualified by 1:5 which underscores his humanity and historicity, 'the faithful witness, the firstborn from the dead and the ruler of kings on earth'.

Here, with great emphasis, three things are said of him. First, to these believers in Roman Asia who are about to enter a time of persecution, John presents Jesus as 'the faithful witness' in that he is the model of how to stand firm in, and never compromise, the truth of God. The Greek word for witness is *martyr*. Originally it simply meant a witness to the truth, a word drawn from the law courts, but because so many Christians died witnessing to the truth of Jesus, martyr became a technical term for someone who gave their life for their testimony. As Bauckham explains, 'The world is a kind of court-room in which the issue of who is the true God is being decided. In this judicial contest Jesus and his followers bear witness to the truth.'[13] Christians who find themselves being called to die for their faith are in good company, that of the 'faithful witness', he is the model they are to follow and in so doing will conquer 'by the blood of the Lamb and by the word of their testimony' (Revelation 12:11).

The second title given to Christ is 'the first-born from the dead'. This is a reference to his resurrection which is the power and guarantee of our own resurrection. Here we have an allusion to Psalm 89:27, 'I will make him the firstborn [Greek *prototokon*], the highest of the kings of the earth.' The overall theme of the psalm is important. It speaks of the Lord's loyalty to David at a time when it seems he has renounced his covenant and his anointed with enemies mocking. The psalmist asks: 'What man can live and never see death? Who can deliver his soul from the power of Sheol [Hades]?' (Psalm 89:48) The answer is given in 1:18, since Jesus is the living one who has 'the keys of Death and Hades'.[14] The rejection of the Messiah and his people is nothing new, what is new is the victory achieved which is to be consummated by Christ at the end of time.

Even now Jesus is the 'ruler of the kings of the earth'. Anyone reading this, other than a Christian, would have thought that John had lost his mind. How can he write to a tiny, threatened, minority group, that Jesus, and not Cæsar, is Lord? He can do so because of his complete confidence in the words and witness of the Lord Jesus and the fact of his risen life and power.

Thirdly, John gives a call to worship the One whose love for sinners had taken him to the cross where he 'freed us from our sins by his blood … To *him* be glory and power for ever and ever! Amen.' (1:5–6, NIV) Jesus freed us from the chains of unbelief and sin and eternal condemnation by bearing that condemnation for us ('the Judge judged in our place' to use the memorable phrase of Karl Barth). He has enabled us to walk free with a new power and new purpose as sons and daughters of God. He has brought us into his world-wide kingdom where we have citizenship, an eternal kingdom, which is eternal life. Jesus can give things no earthly ruler could even dream of giving because of who he is and what he has done: he is the first and the last, the alpha and omega, the beginning and the end.[15]

God the Spirit

Finally we come to the Holy Spirit, rendered here as the 'seven spirits' or the '*sevenfold* Spirit'.[16] He too is the source of grace and peace. The way grace and peace is being given to these people and to us, is by the production of the Book of Revelation itself. To know that Jesus, not Cæsar, is Lord and that this Lord is tender towards us is a wonderful source of grace, giving us a deep and lasting peace. We know the Spirit is involved in this because in 1:10 we are told that John was '*in the Spirit*' when he received this prophecy. At the end of each letter a church fellowship is exhorted, 'hear what the *Spirit* says to the churches' i.e. listen to what he is saying through *this* book. This book is the Spirit's gift to his people and is to be read and treasured as such: 'We owe to the Scriptures the same reverence as we owe to God, since it has its only source in Him and has nothing of human origin mixed with it.'[17]

Not only is the Spirit the one who brings this prophecy about, he also tenderly applies it to our souls bringing the grace and peace of God from the throne of God; he is God dwelling *with* and working *in* us.

The fact that the Spirit doesn't get the same extended treatment as the Father and the Son do in this passage does not indicate lack of importance. It actually underscores the Spirit's intention *not* to draw attention to himself, but rather to glorify the Son (who glorifies the Father): 'He will glorify me, for he will take what is mine and declare it to you' (John 16:14). The way he strengthens us is by working in us as we read the Book of Revelation (which he has declared to John), thus enabling us to keep looking to the Father and the Son and in so doing becoming more like them.

Richard Sibbes describes this work of the Spirit as follows:

> The very beholding of Christ is a transforming sight. The Spirit that makes us new creatures and stirs us up to behold this servant [Jesus], it is a *transforming* beholding … A man cannot look upon the love of God and of Christ in the Gospel, without it changing him to be like God and Christ. For how can he see Christ and God in Christ, but also see how God hates sin, and this will transform us to hate it as God does, who hated it so that it could not be expiated but with the blood of Christ, the God-man. So, seeing the holiness of God in it, it will transform us to be holy. When we see the love of God in the Gospel, and the love of Christ giving himself for us, this will transform us to love God.'[18]

Isn't that your experience? The more you look at Jesus the more you want to become like him and are gradually made like him? That is the Spirit at work.

Re-enchantment

In chapter one we saw how the prevailing 'social

imaginary' in which people live and move and have their being is secular. One of the tragic results of the secularisation process is what Max Weber calls disenchantment (*Entzauberung*), where the 'magic' or 'mystery' of life is not just removed, but unwanted. We are simply to apply reason and technology with the consequence that matters of faith are deemed irrelevant. This occurs at a societal level. But it can also occur on a more personal level, affecting Christians. Contrasting the way children and adults view things, David Bentley Hart writes:

> As we age ... we lose our sense of the intimate otherness of things; we allow habit to displace awe, inevitably to banish delight; we grow into adulthood and "put away childish things" ... Thereafter, there are only fleeting instants carried throughout our lives when all at once, our defences are momentarily relaxed, we find ourselves brought to pause by a sudden unanticipated sense of the uncanniness of the reality we inhabit, the startling fortuity and strangeness of everything familiar; how odd it is, and how unfathomable, that anything at all exists; how disconcerting that the world and one's consciousness of it are simply there, joined in a single ineffable event.[19]

One of the hoped for consequences for Christians reading the Book of Revelation is a recapturing of a child-like enchantment with 'all things, visible and invisible' and the triune God who made, sustains and redeems them. As we reverently bow before each member of the Trinity as displayed through the pages of the Apocalypse, may it be our experience that awe is rekindled and delight reawakened, that the vibrant world John saw, which contrasts so starkly with the grey, eviscerated world of many of our contemporaries, may be the world our churches inhabit as they delight more and more in the Trinity.

3. God the Father of Revelation

AFTER THE UNIMAGINABLE SLAUGHTER OF THE FIRST World War and the beginning of the Irish War for Independence, W.B. Yeats wrote a poem entitled, 'The Second Coming' which began:

> Turning and turning in the widening gyre
> The falcon cannot hear the falconer;
> Things fall apart; the centre cannot hold;
> Mere anarchy is loosed upon the world,
> The blood-dimmed tide is loosed, and everywhere
> The ceremony of innocence is drowned;
> The best lack all conviction, while the worst
> Are full of passionate intensity.

'Things fall apart; the centre cannot hold' — that appears to be an accurate description of our world. When there is no centre to hold things together, things simply fall apart. They fall apart in a country if there is no effective government. They fall apart in a family if there are no parents. They fall apart in an individual if there is no centre of meaning in their soul. Things fall apart.

That is certainly the way things appear to be from our perspective. However, in the Apocalypse, God, through his Son the Lord Jesus Christ, gives his servant John a vision to show to his people and the world. The vision says, if they are only willing to listen, that there *is* a centre which holds everything together. The centre is not imperial Rome, despite its propaganda to the contrary. What lies at the heart of the universe is a throne and most significantly the One who rules from that throne. In his triune glory, the majestic Lord holds *everything* together; from the furthest stars in the outer galaxies, to the smallest sparrow in the garden and most importantly of all, his tiny, persecuted people, the church. We see this in all its dazzling splendour and earth shaking power in Revelation chapter 4.

The Book of Revelation refers to God's throne nearly forty times including twelve times in this chapter, underscoring its vital importance. Furthermore, the whole of creation finds its significance in being rightly oriented towards this throne. Everything in the vision is introduced in relation to the throne: the sevenfold Spirit and the sea of glass are *before* the throne. A rainbow, twenty-four thrones and the elders are positioned *around* the throne. The four living creatures are in the *midst* of the throne.

And flashes of lightning, rumblings and peals of thunder emanate *from* the throne.

Today, thrones don't have much of a place in people's lives. You may see a throne in a museum from some ancient culture. And where they do have a place, such as in Great Britain for example, they tend only to have a ceremonial role or symbolic role, the Queen bestowing a knighthood and the like. However, once things were very different. There was a time when thrones radiated meaning. They symbolised the sovereign's authority and will. It was from thrones that societies were shaped and declarations made. Thrones stood for power, wealth, sometimes justice and always entitlement to *rule*. This is the image we are being presented with here, but purged of all its human imperfections — the rule of God.[1]

We have been seeing that the most effective antidote for Christians to resist the pressures to believe the lies around them is to get a proper grip on reality. This is what the Book of Revelation provides. In the Apocalypse a 'lifting the veil' takes place, giving believers access to the unseen, ultimate reality which is God on his throne.

What is immediately striking upon reading this and the next chapter is that we enter a world of *order*. This is not the order of a prison, but the order of a palace, a place of awe-inspiring beauty and safety. As de Silva reminds us, the visions of chapters 4 and 5 extend the 'conceptual map' of reality outward into 'the realm beyond the visible heavens, figuratively accessed through a door which must crack open the dome of the sky before mortals can observe the activity and personnel in that realm.'[2]

A cursory glance at the heavenly throne room reveals that everything and everyone are in their rightful place. It is by being so located that everything finds its significance and functions rightly.

First and foremost, God sits enthroned in the midst of concentric circles of heavenly beings. The four living creatures, resembling the cherubim and seraphim — angelic attendants (4:6–8; cf. Isaiah 6:2–3; Ezekiel 1:5–11) — move about the throne in tight orbit. Twenty-four elders sit upon thrones, arranged around the divine throne and facing it. Around these, in an ever-widening circle, are the myriad angelic hosts (5:11). All the superhuman creatures give their undivided attention to God and the Lamb and are caught up in constant praise. At the furthest reaches of this cosmic map John positions, 'every creature in heaven and on earth and under the earth and in the sea' (5:13), united in the worship of God.

This is important for two reasons

First, life in general, and sometimes the Christian life in particular, can be experienced as chaotic:

> So a family loses its young mother to breast cancer while, a block away, neighbours are rolling with laughter at a television comedy. A middle-aged man despondently leaves his office for the last time, retired early with blank indifference, while outside on the

street people are just strolling by. Or a torturer's victim spits out blood from his battered mouth while in the café next door to the police station, two lovers are gazing into each other's eyes over a glass of wine. Life just goes on. The cries of our hearts are unheard, and the loneliness adds to the pain.[3]

For many Christians living under the oppressive heel of Domitian at the time of John's Revelation, just as many Christians living in North Korea are now experiencing, their world of security and order was being replaced by threat and uncertainty. But the vision of chapters 4 and 5 show that even the present chaos is temporary and relative and is to be placed within the wider context of God's ordering of the universe.[4]

Secondly, order and peace were claimed to lie within the gift of the Roman Emperor. This was the celebrated '*Pax Romana*', the 'peace of Rome' which began with Augustus in 27 BC for which the citizens of the Empire were meant to be truly grateful. This gratitude was to be expressed in public celebrations:

Imperial temples and sanctuaries were wreathed with flowers. Animals were sacrificed at various altars throughout the main locations of the city, for example, the council house, temples of other deities, theatres, the main squares, stadiums, and gymnasiums. These political, religious, and public buildings were linked together by processions and dignitaries, garlanded animals being led to slaughter, and bearers of icons and symbols of the emperor. As the procession passed by, householders would sacrifice on small altars outside their homes. The whole city thus had opportunity to join in the celebration.[5]

By such devices 'peace' and 'order' were to be celebrated and were designed to inspire awe towards the Emperor as well as express thankfulness. This was what ordinary Christians had to witness on a regular basis (all the seven cities addressed by John in Asia Minor had cultic sites devoted to the imperial cult of which Pergamum was the chief). John's vision of the heavenly celebration of the genuine guarantor of peace and order exposes the arrogance of Rome for the sham that it was.

What follows is not to be separated from the previous three chapters and the situations of the local congregations:

> The vision that unfolds is the answer to all the questions and issues raised up till now, and the picture of the power and majesty of God sets the wider context that all the followers of Jesus need to see as their own. Why worry about temporary opposition, either from Jews or pagans, if God is truly enthroned and all-powerful? Why compromise with surrounding culture when the patterns of authority there are just a shadow of the reality of God's authority? And why falter and stumble if this vision represents your inheritance and your destiny?[6]

There are three things which we encounter as, with John, we enter the heavenly throne room.

The supremacy of God

> After this I looked, and behold, a door standing open in heaven! And the first voice, which I had heard speaking to me like a trumpet, said, "Come up here, and I will show you what must take place after this." At once I was in the Spirit, and behold, a throne stood in heaven, with one seated on the throne. And he who sat there had the appearance of jasper and carnelian, and around the throne was a rainbow that had the appearance of an emerald. (4:1–3)

God is never described as such, because, apart from the fact that God is spirit and can't be seen, he is infinite and therefore indescribable. To be sure there is *someone* seated on the throne ruling, but he can't easily be captured by words. Thus he is described as having the *appearance* of jasper and the *appearance* of ruby and so on. God himself is never directly described; it is always in terms of the 'likeness of' and never 'this is what he *is*'.

This is a very important principle to bear in mind when thinking about God and the kind of language to be used about him. There are two extremes to be avoided, both of which have catastrophic examples in church history.

At one pole there is language which attempts to describe God as if we know *exactly* what he is like; this is speaking of God *univocally*, such that the meaning of one thing is the same as the meaning of something else. Those who claim that it is not helpful to think of God as 'Father' because of the poor experience some have had of earthly fathers fall into this trap. In whatever manner God is to be conceived as 'Father' it is not in every respect like human fathers.

At the other end of the spectrum is what is called *equivocal* knowledge, maintaining that God is so *unlike* anything or anyone that nothing can reasonably be said about him. This is the route of sceptism or subjectivism, such that 'God is whatever he/she/it means to me, since we can't know anything about God objectively.'[7]

The language of the Bible, and the Book of Revelation, is the much more guarded language of *analogy*. To say that a thing is 'analogical' is to say that something shares *some* similarities with something else but cannot be too closely identified with it. This is the language of John with his qualified 'in the likeness of' and 'having the appearance of' terminology. This means that because of God's self-revelation we *can* know God truly if not exhaustively.[8]

The description we are given of the one who occupies this throne is simply breathtaking. This is precisely the effect it is intended to have. The One seated there is like jasper which is white and sparkles like a diamond; and ruby or carnelian, which is fiery red, and emerald — a glittering green. 'The stones intensify the light around the throne by reflecting the unapproachable brightness, and hence glory, surrounding God himself.'[9]

The rainbow could mean the vertical multi-coloured bow we see in the sky after rain or something horizontal, more like a halo or the rings of the planet Saturn. Of course the rainbow takes us back to the sign given by God after the flood, a sign that he is a faithful and merciful God who restores order after the chaos of judgement (9:13). Taken together the effect is to evoke an image of pure, entrancing beauty.

The nearest thing I have experienced like this was when my wife and I travelled to Norway to see the Northern Lights. You slowly make your journey towards the cold wilderness beneath a black sky, studded with stars, then, very faintly at first, you see a green glow dancing on the horizon. This then begins to gleam with greater intensity and the dance of the lights becomes all the more elaborate. This is followed by what appears to be a giant green and yellow curtain shimmering over the mountains, and then suddenly the configuration changes into a green and yellow crown with flecks of red forming directly overhead. This display goes on and on and, what is more, you never tire of it. Your mind is left racing with the mesmerising beauty of it all. I remember thinking this must be what it will be like when we enter into heaven. John's experience is something like that, but heightened to an entirely different level of spiritual and emotional intensity because God reigns supreme.

The holiness of God

The Bible never defines holiness as such, especially when applied to God; rather, it is a term which in many respects signifies the *otherness* of God, the *Godness* of God if you will, how he is so utterly and wholly *unlike* us in his divine attributes. It is a term often associated with the radiance of God (*Shekinah*), which far outshines anything we could imagine. It is sometimes linked to *glory*, the *weight* of God (*kabod*), which outweighs the entire cosmos. The absolute, transcendent, otherness of God — his holiness — is conveyed in the vision of chapter 4 in several ways.

First, by the way the divine throne is enhanced by spectacular heavenly beings: 'Around the throne were twenty-four thrones, and seated on the thrones were twenty-four elders, clothed in white garments, with golden crowns on their heads' (4:4).

There is some debate regarding the identity of the elders, whether they are angelic beings, which is the interpretation I prefer.[10] The focus however, is not so much *what* they are but *who* they represent. They are wearing crowns indicating rule, and dressed in white which is the colour of victory. Their number, twenty-four, has representative function. So it would seem these figures represent before the throne of God the entire people of God — the *twelve* tribes of Israel in the Old Testament and the *twelve* apostles in the New — symbolising 'the entire community of the redeemed of both testaments'.[11]

One implication of this is that God's people are never without supernatural representatives in heaven, so they are never out of God's mind for a single moment. That indicates how God values us; he has so arranged the courtroom of heaven to ensure we are never forgotten. Not that God is capable of forgetting! Rather, the symbolism is of advocates in a royal court. It would be of great comfort for a citizen of an ancient country to know that he had a representative before the King. How much more is it consoling to know that we are always before the King of kings? In other words, the arrangement is for our benefit.

The crowns and the clothing symbolise kingship and victory. The suffering Christians of Asia Minor are to see themselves and their martyred companions in this light. They may have suffered on earth but they reign in heaven, they may have been despised here, but are honoured there. Christians belonging to John's churches can look from a Roman prison or a slave mine to the throne room of God and with the eyes of faith see this. In short, what we are shown is a picture of the church *in* heaven. This is the way Greg Beale describes it:

> The church is pictured in *angelic* guise to remind its members that already a dimension of their existence is heavenly, that their real home is not with the unbelieving "earth-dwellers", and that they have heavenly help and protection in their struggle to obtain their reward and not be conformed to their pagan environment.

He goes on,

> One of the purposes of the church meeting on earth in its weekly gatherings (as in 1:3, 9) is to be reminded of its heavenly existence and identity by modelling its worship and liturgy on the angels' and the heavenly

church's worship of the exalted lamb, as vividly portrayed in chapters 4–5.[12]

One of the reasons for a church fellowship meeting each week is so they can have this kind of perspective renewed and strengthened. Christians are meant to see their lives, careers, years of strength and days of weakness in *this* light and having *this* significance. This is where we shall *be* one day; this is where we now *belong* in principle. It is our true home. Even as Christians meet together in whatever building might be available to them, at the same time they meet in the divine throne room, which extends to their feet as they worship.

The awe inspiring holiness of God is emphasised even more forcefully by the next few images:

> From the throne came flashes of lightning, and rumblings and peals of thunder, and before the throne were burning seven torches of fire, which are the seven spirits of God, and before the throne there was as it were a sea of glass, like crystal. (4:5–6)

There are three images in this passage. First, there is the *lightning and the thunder*. In the days before the nuclear bomb, a thunderstorm would have been one of the most powerful, destructive forces the ancients knew. Not the rather tame storms we tend to have in the United Kingdom, but the dark, wild, booming electrical storms which stalk the great continents where, when thunder erupts, the whole ground shakes, and when lightning strikes the whole sky is lit up. When God met with his people at Sinai, *this* is what they saw and they were terrified. Nature in the raw, nature unleashed at its most violent: that indicates what encircles the throne of God. To think that one can blithely walk into the presence of this God would be as suicidal as walking into an atomic blast — it can't be done!

Secondly, there are *the seven lamps*, a reflection of the sevenfold spirit, signifying the perfection of God's *Holy Spirit*; perfect in wisdom, righteousness, and power. This brings home the truth that the way God's presence *can* be mediated to us is by His Spirit, but in such a way that God still keeps a certain distance. He can meet us on earth while still remaining in heaven.

Thirdly there is the *sea of glass, clear as crystal*. This is significant for at least two reasons. First, it appears to create *an insuperable barrier*. How is John, who is watching all of this, ever, if at all, going to get close to the throne? He looks and before him is a sea of glass which is vast; then he observes the sevenfold spirit which mediates whatever there is of God to his creation; next is the blinding storm which hides God; then concentric ranks of angels and archangels and even after that he can see God in such a way that can only be spoken of in terms of metaphor and simile. How do you approach such a God who is completely and terrifyingly holy? What is needed is some sort of protection, a kind of 'go-between', someone who will be able to bridge the gap of infinity and introduce us to God such that intimacy can be achieved without compromising God's purity or bringing about our demise. The good news is that such a one exists and will be introduced in the next chapter — the Lion who is the Lamb.

Secondly, we are to note that it is a *sea* of glass, *clear as crystal*. In the Bible the sea often depicts chaos, rebellion and turmoil (think of the flood in Genesis 7 when there was a return to the primeval chaos of Genesis 1:1; or the threat the Red Sea posed to the Hebrews as they were pursued by Pharaoh's armies; or the power and threat of the waves described in Psalm 89:9). The sea is dark and unruly, churning sediment, delivering up debris, detritus and even dead bodies onto its shores. Isaiah brings these images together, 'The wicked are like the tossing sea, which cannot rest, whose waves cast up mire and mud' (Isaiah 57:20). This depicts the effects of Satan's works in the world, as we shall see in chapter 13, as well as being a picture of the world organised in opposition to God. This is why on earth things seem so uncertain and unpredictable, with economic meltdowns, wars, and famines (the stuff of chapter 6–9). As a result we are tossed about like flotsam and jetsam and become disorientated by it all. But for God, and from where he rules, there is no such sea, a sea of rebellion and uncertainty. The sea that exists before him is as smooth and as solid as a sheet of glass. It is also as clear as crystal, wholly transparent so there is nothing sinister lurking in its depths, no Leviathan ready to leap out and do damage. It is a great comfort to know this is so. One day, as the last chapters of Revelation show, the *whole* of creation will be in this state ('there was no sea') when his kingdom comes and his will is done on earth as in heaven. God is completely composed and completely in control.

The worship of God

> And around the throne, on each side of the throne, are four living creatures, full of eyes in front and behind: the first living creature like a lion, the second living creature like an ox, the third living creature with the face of a man, and the fourth living creature like an eagle in flight. (4:6b–7)

Often ancient thrones were constructed so they looked as if they rested on creatures. For example, King Solomon had lions' heads protruding from his throne (1 Kings 10:20), and we see something like that here. These creatures, however, have characteristics of the highest order of angels, the cherubim. They have wings and different faces representing different aspects of God. One is like a lion, a symbol of royalty; one, an ox, a symbol of strength; another, the face of a man, indicating intelligence; and still another, an eagle, having the ability to act swiftly. All these attributes find their perfection in God. Not only do these creatures enhance God's throne and co-ordinate praise to the one seated on the throne, but their symbolism suggests that God's throne rests on *royal decree*; he alone has the wisdom to do what is perfectly right, the power to bring it about and to do so swiftly, at the right time and in the right way for the sake of his people.

In the original Greek the emphasis is not so much on who these creatures *are* but on what they are *doing*, namely, worship: 'Day and night they never stop saying: "Holy, holy, holy is the Lord God Almighty, who was, and is, and is to come"' (4:8, NIV)) The closer you get to God, the more praise there is: the four living creatures constantly praise him, and then the whole of heaven gets caught up in the chorus of praise as we see in 4:9–11:

> And whenever the living creatures give glory and honour and thanks to him who is seated on the throne, who lives forever and ever, the twenty-four elders fall down before him who is seated on the throne and worship him who lives forever and ever. They cast their crowns before the throne, saying, "Worthy are you, our Lord and God, to receive glory and honour and power for you created all things, and by your will they existed and were created."

We should take note of the fact that the twenty-four elders, the beings that represent the community of faith, take up the worship: 'In casting down their crowns before the throne the elders acknowledge that their authority is a delegated authority. The honour given to them is freely returned to the One who alone is worthy of universal honour.'[13] This stands in striking contrast to the Roman Emperors who saw themselves as worthy of wearing their crowns. According to Josephus, Vespasian was hailed as benefactor and saviour; the only 'worthy' ruler of Rome.[14] The reality is quite different: there is only one who is worthy of such tireless devotion and he occupies the throne of heaven.

Let God be God

In contrast to the Cæsar worship of John's day and the cult of celebrity of our day, the worship which lies at the heart of the universe, and which undergirds all reality, is singularly lacking any man-centeredness. Indeed, 'humanity is radically displaced from the centre of things where human beings naturally place themselves.'[15] Genuine, lasting worship is theocentric not anthropocentric. Even here in the celestial worship human beings are not pre-eminent. It is the four living creatures who initiate and lead the worship of heaven in 4:8; only the third of these has a human face. They represent worship on behalf of *all* creatures. The circle of worship is not complete until it is embraced by 'every creature in heaven and on earth and under the earth and in the sea' (5:13).

What the great throne room of Revelation 4 declares, loud and clear, is that God *is* God. He is the centre, not us. He is infinite, we are finite. He is self-existent, we are dependent.

> All spiritualities that begin within the self, building on the self as their religious source, are false. The self cannot reach out, in, or up and find God in a redemptive way. All of these cultural spiritualities have assumed that the boundary set between the Creator and creature, between a holy God and sinners, can be

crossed from our side and crossed naturally and easily. It cannot. Only God, the infinite Creator and the one who is utterly holy can cross these boundaries. They are crossed only from "above" and they can only be crossed by God himself. He rules: we are ruled. He acts: we are acted upon. He gives life: we receive it … We live in his world. He is not, therefore an intruder in our world. In short, he is above and we are below.[16]

Worship is the great activity of heaven. It is not vacuous and non-specific, it is rich and full of content, consumed with the nature and being of God as Creator-Redeemer. Worship is the rightful response of creatures to their Creator. If that is the case in heaven, it should also be so on earth, worshipping God in 'spirit and in truth' (John 4:24). Without it the 'centre will not hold'. It is in this worship that we take our rightful place in the world and do so joyfully. When God is at the centre then everything changes; we discover *what* we were made for and *who* we were made for, to know and worship God. Worship isn't something vague and insubstantial:

Worship is eminently practical because adoring and affectionate praise is what restores our sense of ultimate value. It exposes the worthless and temporary and tawdry stuff of this world. Worship energises the heart to seek satisfaction in Jesus alone. In worship we are reminded that this world is fleeting and unworthy of our heart's devotion. Worship connects our souls with the transcendent power of God and awakens in us appreciation for true beauty. It pulls back the veil of deception and exposes the ugliness of sin and Satan. Worship is a joyful rebuke of the world. When our hearts are riveted on Jesus everything else in life becomes so utterly unnecessary and we become far less demanding.[17]

In other words, we become better people: more contented people, people who are easier to live with, people with a purpose because we have come to know the one who is of supreme worth. In fact we start to do on earth what the twenty-four elders do in heaven, we lay our crowns, symbols of rule, before God's throne and in so doing joyfully acknowledge his saving, loving, soul-satisfying rule. We are not to settle for anything less.

4. God the Son of Revelation

BISHOP FESTO KIVENGERE OF UGANDA WAS KNOWN AS THE 'Billy Graham of Africa.' He once said: 'Please don't be shocked if you hear that there is a revolution in Burundi, Uganda or Zaire. This is Africa! It's nothing when young countries get revolution. They are going to get some more. But that doesn't mean that the Man of Galilee has vacated the throne! Christianity has never been scared of a revolution. Satan can roar like a lion, but he has no authority to shake the throne on which Jesus is sitting.' The apostle John would have agreed wholeheartedly with that sentiment because he had *seen* the throne on which the ascended Lord Jesus was sitting which was nothing less than the throne of God.

However, at first sight things don't look too promising. Heaven, which we would presume to be a place of delight, turns out, in John's experience in the first instance, to be a place of despair.

A desperate need

> Then I saw in the right hand of him who was seated
> on the throne a scroll written within and on the back,
> sealed with seven seals. And I saw a mighty angel
> proclaiming with a loud voice, "Who is worthy to open
> the scroll and break its seals?" And no one in heaven or
> on earth or under the earth was able to open the scroll
> or to look into it, and I began to weep loudly because
> no one was found worthy to open the scroll or to look
> into it. (5:1–4)

This is still part of the first vision while John was 'in the
Spirit' which began in chapter 4. It is the divine throne
room with God reigning in ineffable majesty; wholly
transcendent.

This 'distancing' of God raises some serious questions:
how can creatures like ourselves, sinful and finite, ever
know the God who is holy and infinite such that we can
have fellowship with him and he with us? How can God
achieve his saving purposes on earth in a way that is just
without consigning a wayward humanity to oblivion?

It is at this point that we see a development of the
dazzling splendour of chapter 4 into the breathtaking
drama of chapter 5. It's as if the camera zooms in for a
close up shot of the right hand of the one who sits on his
exalted throne, the right hand being the symbol of regal
authority, the 'right hand of power'. What John sees being
held in that hand is a scroll sealed with seven seals. The
question is: what is its significance?

Some point out that in the first century Roman wills were witnessed and sealed by seven witnesses, the contents of such a will was sometimes summarised on the back and a trustworthy executor would then put the will into effect. Others propose that it fits contracts and deeds in Roman society at this time whose contents were written on inner pages which were folded and sealed, usually with seven seals. The contents were also indicated in full or in summary on the back or outer sheet. Whatever the precise details, this appears to be a legal contract of some kind.

However, scrolls have prophetic precedent, and this is, after all, a prophecy (1:3). When we take note of the fact that in both Daniel and Ezekiel scrolls 'have to do principally with events of judgment, which are then followed by the salvation of God's people' as suggested by Beale, then his conclusion is one which commends itself: 'The "book"' is 'best understood as God's plan of judgment and redemption', a plan 'which has been set in motion by Christ's death and resurrection but has yet to be completed'.[1] In other words, this is a legal document which represents the sum total of God's purposes for redemption and judgement. It is the heavenly King's royal decree in written form.

Breaking the seals and opening the scroll are not references to the mere reading of God's plan but to *carrying* it out. It is fulfilling the divine intent, the executing of the divine plan of judgment and redemption. Until those seals are broken and the contents of the document revealed, then none of this can be done. Who, then, has the executive power to put into effect God's will on earth? Is there *anyone* who is both qualified and capable? That was the cry of the angel.

We are told he was a *mighty* angel and proclaimed in a *loud* voice. Before the days of amplification systems the only way an announcement could be made and heard by large numbers was by having some sort of 'Town Crier'. Here is the angelic equivalent. The desperate call goes out from one end of the cosmos to the other. The voice echoes like cosmic thunder throughout the universe: 'Who is worthy to put into operation the saving work of God in sinful human history? Who is worthy to assume sovereignty over the destiny of millions? Who is worthy to lift the terrible burden of guilt and push back the powers of evil and establish the eternal kingdom of God?' That is in effect what is being asked through this angelic herald.

Silence and despair

The answering silence is one of the two great silences in the Book of Revelation (the other being when the seventh and final seal is opened in 8:1). Amongst all the angels and archangels, prophets and priests, together with all the world's spiritual leaders, religions and philosophers, there is *not a single person to be found*. Perhaps we can now begin to appreciate why John weeps, feeling as if he is trapped in some kind of celestial nightmare. What thoughts might have been passing through his mind at this point? Perhaps: 'Is this how it will always be in the world, with no protection for God's children in the hours of bitter trial; no judgments upon a persecuting world; no ultimate triumph for believers; no new heaven and earth; no future inheritance? What of the cruelty of the Emperor, will that never be avenged? Is righteousness for ever to be excluded from God's world?' It certainly seems that way, *if* there is no one to open the scroll to carry out God's righteous will — hence the bitter tears of despair.

Despair was the prevailing mood amongst artists and intellectuals for much of the twentieth century. In one of his more reflective moods Woody Allen said:

> The fundamental thing behind all motivation and all activity is the constant struggle against annihilation and against death. It's absolutely stupefying in its terror, and it renders anyone's accomplishments meaningless. As Camus wrote, it's not only that he the individual dies, or that man as a whole dies, but that you struggle to do a work of art that will last and then you realise that the universe itself is not going to exist after a period of time.'[2]

What is Woody Allen's answer? We create our own fake meaning:

> The universe is indifferent ... so we create a fake world for ourselves, and we exist within that fake world ... a world that, in fact, means nothing at all, when you step back. It's meaningless. But it's important that we create some sense of meaning, because no perceptible meaning exists for anybody.[3]

There is, however, a solution. Not fabricating a fake

universe like Allen, but being exposed to the real universe as God has made it and submitting to the one for whom it was created. This was to be John's experience and it could be ours.

Divine provision

It is the voice of one of the elders (the higher order of angels) which provides the reassuring answer to the angelic cry: 'And one of the elders said to me, "Weep no more; behold, the Lion of the tribe of Judah, the Root of David, has conquered, so that he can open the scroll and its seven seals"' (5:5).

John, being familiar with the Old Testament, would have immediately known who the Lion of the tribe of Judah, the root of David, was. Genesis 49:9 speaks of the tribe of Judah being a 'lion's cub', that is, from this tribe would come God's appointed ruler. Similarly in Isaiah 11:1 the promise is made that a shoot would 'come forth' which would also be from the root of David, who will 'stand as a banner for the peoples; the nations will rally to him' (11:10, NIV). This is Messianic language. And this is the one who can take the scroll and put into effect God's decrees. What qualifies him for this task is because he has *triumphed*. The Greek word suggests a victorious struggle which qualifies him for this unique role, having done that which the readers of several of the letters have been urged to do, namely, 'conquer' (e.g. 2:7). Exactly what that struggle was we discover next, as John lifts his head to look for this Lion only to see a Lamb!

> And between the throne and the four living creatures
> and among the elders I saw a Lamb standing, as though
> it had been slain, with seven horns and with seven eyes,
> which are the seven spirits of God sent out into all the
> earth. (5:6)

This 'human Lamb' which John sees is 'standing in the centre of the throne'. This probably means he is positioned in the space no angel could ever occupy, standing on the *God-side* of all authority and standing *with* God in the centre of the circle of angelic worship. Jesus is no 'god' in any diminished sense, he *is* God, otherwise he would not occupy this divine space. Neither is he merely the God of Christians, since he is the One by which everything was made and for whom it was made, which is indicated in this vision by the universal worship he receives (cf. Colossians 1:16). The Lamb is the rightful sovereign over all people whether they realise it or not, or care to acknowledge it or not. The fact that many are in rebellion against him doesn't make him any less their ruler; in some ways their rebellion underscores the terrible nature of their lawlessness, that they should spurn someone who is as kind and as glorious as this.

'The key to John's vision of the slaughtered Lamb … is to recognise the contrast between what he hears (5:5) and what he sees (5:6).'[4] On the one hand, titles such as the 'Lion of Judah' would have had strong militaristic associations, whereas on the other hand, talk of a 'slain Lamb' speaks of innocence. The result is a reinterpretation of Messianic hopes, that God's victory *is* achieved but through a sacrificial death (cf. Jesus' own teaching in Mark 10:45), 'Thus Jesus fulfils Old Testament prophesies of messianic kingship in an ironic and surprising way.'[5] Similarly Thomas Schreiner writes:

> It is abundantly clear that the lion triumphs as the lamb, that victory comes not through destroying one's enemies but rather through suffering for their sake and for their salvation. Judgement will come, but there is a reprieve for those who believe and repent because the lamb has suffered for their sake.[6]

The declaration of the existence of the all-conquering Lion of Judah is displaced by a vision of a slaughtered Lamb.

Characteristics of the Lamb

There are two things to note in particular with regards to the Lamb. First, it is a *sacrificial* lamb, like the ones used during the Exodus to ensure that the Angel of Death passed over God's people (Exodus 12:3–6). It is also not possible to miss the association with the lamb-like servant of Isaiah 53:7.

What is more, it is a *powerful* lamb, having seven horns, symbols of princely strength (Daniel 7:24; 8:21–22) and seven eyes which are the 'seven spirits of God', indicating omniscience (all knowledge) and omnisapience (all wisdom) (Zechariah 4:10; Isaiah 11:2; cf. Revelation 1:4). Neither should it be overlooked that omniscient ability is something which belongs to Yahweh *alone,* rendering him fit to execute the judgement: 'I [Yahweh] search the heart and test the mind, to give every man according to his ways, according to the fruit of his deeds' (Jeremiah 17:10). In this vision, that ability is ascribed to the Lamb which is a further indication of his divine nature.

These two attributes of the Lamb would have been of particular relevance to John and his readers undergoing hardship and persecution because of their allegiance to Christ.

From hopelessness to hope

When facing difficulty certain pressing questions come to the fore: 'What is to become of Christian believers who appear subject to unseen spiritual powers often operating through political structures? Will they be crushed between conflicting forces or swallowed up by world events?' The answer is 'no' because this One has the knowledge and insight of God as well as the power and might of God to protect and preserve his people. He can strengthen because he is strong; he can see who needs help because he is all-seeing, 'For the eyes of the LORD range throughout the earth to strengthen those whose hearts are fully committed to him' (2 Chronicles 16:9, NIV). This is the message of the horns and the eyes of the exalted Lamb. He strengthens by sending his Holy Spirit who is pictured as 'the *seven* Spirits of God' not because there are seven Holy Spirits but because he is the *perfect* Spirit of God, complete in all the power and goodness of the Godhead.

In this one vision we are being presented with the triune

God: Father, Son and Holy Spirit in complete control over everything, working together *in* all things for the sake of the people for whom the Lamb of God was slain, in order to save (cf. Romans 8:28). If God has gone to such lengths for his people, there can be no greater lengths to which he will not go to preserve them. Jesus is now Lord of the Spirit; the Spirit of God is his 'everywhere-agent', which means there will be no failure of communication or operation.

It is also important to notice where the Lamb comes from, namely the *throne* itself, he is *already* standing at the centre of the throne; he doesn't have to approach it. The significance of this spatial imagery is that it is God, in the person of his Son, who takes the initiative to execute salvation and judgement.

A problem to be faced

God has to deal with the fundamental cause of the rot in his world, which is sin. This vision, and especially that of the 'bloodied Lamb', should bring home to us the seriousness of sin in the light of the holiness of God. We are back to the much needed 'social imaginary' of the Bible, the lens through which to see the world as it really is. It was the historian Herbert Butterfield who perceptively said, 'If we imagine the world of generally righteous men with — at any given moment — only one especially wicked nation in it, we shall never envisage the seriousness of that situation with which Christianity sets out to deal.'[7] The Book of Revelation disabuses us of such

Pollyanna optimism and presents the world as God sees it and as Christians *should* see it.

All that corrupts and separates us from him has to be settled. God cannot do this by mere 'say so' from heaven. He has to step down from the throne into the grime and muck of our world in order to deal with it. The Lion has to *become* the Lamb (without ceasing to be the Lion) so we can be saved. Why?

The Lion as the Lamb — God becomes man

The early church faced the heresy of Arianism (the great-grandfather of the Jehovah's Witnesses) which argued that Jesus was 'like' God, but was not of the same substance *as* God (i.e. he did not share the throne as depicted in Revelation 5). In this controversy the church saw clearly that the identity and mission of Jesus were intertwined: the Lion had to *become* the Lamb. The great Athanasius (AD 296–376) followed through the logic of salvation as presented in the Bible. Only God can save (Isaiah 46:3), so Jesus must be God to fulfil this necessary condition, or he is no Saviour at all. If God has been personally offended by man then God must personally forgive those offences against him. This can't be delegated to another, God himself must do this. Furthermore, since it is man who has done the offending there needs to be a man who will represent man. The result is the need for someone who is both God *and* man, and the biblical testimony is that Jesus Christ meets both requirements. The second person of the Holy Trinity steps down from his heavenly throne to become the sacrificial Lamb in order to lift people up to the throne of heaven.[8]

In 5:7, John says of the all-powerful and omniscient Lamb, 'he went and took the scroll from the right hand of him who was seated on the throne.' The taking possession of the scroll is the sign that he had taken sovereign authority over the future of the human race for judgment and redemption.

Here is the answer to the question: how is God working out his eternal decree in the world? It is through Christ, who has been given executive power by the Father to enact his will on earth in saving and judging, and will do both perfectly. This is what is sometimes referred to as God's mediatorial kingdom.[9]

Earlier I mentioned Bishop Festo Kivengere who used to tell this, his favourite story: 'One day a little girl sat watching her mother working in the kitchen. She asked her mummy, "What does God do all day long?" For a while the mother was stumped, but then she said, "Darling, I'll tell you what God does all day long. He spends his whole day mending broken things."'[10] That is what the triune God is doing, mending broken things like you and me and ultimately a broken world.

A dramatic response

The moment the Lamb takes the scroll to enact God's will there is spontaneous and unsolicited worship:

... the four living creatures and the twenty-four elders

fell down before the Lamb, each holding a harp, and golden bowls full of incense, which are the prayers of the saints. And they sang a new song, saying, "Worthy are you to take the scroll and to open its seals, for you were slain, and by your blood you ransomed people for God from every tribe and language and people and nation and you have made them a kingdom and priests to our God, and they shall reign on the earth." (5:8–10)

The four living creatures and the elders, who have previously been prostrate before the one seated on the throne, now offer exactly the *same* worship to the Lamb as they did to God! The two figures of the one seated on the throne and the Lamb standing in the midst of the throne characterise God as creator and redeemer. The two are never merged because if they were it would mean there is one being but in two guises, sometimes God appearing as Father, sometimes as Son, which is the heresy of modalism or Sabellianism. There is only *one* God as there is only *one* throne, but occupied by *two* persons who share the *same* divine nature. These together with the sevenfold Spirit who proceeds from Christ is the Trinity.

Powerful praise

It was customary in the first century to stand for prayer, both in Graeco-Roman practice as well as for Jews and Christians. This prostration therefore demonstrates extreme reverence or urgent supplication. The four living creatures representing the perfections of God reflected in what he has made, and the twenty-four elders, the angelic creatures representing the whole people of God, sing a new song. This is a new *kind* of song (Greek *koine*) in the sense that all of God's creative and saving purposes now find their climax and consummation in Jesus Christ:

> Worthy are you to take the scroll and to open its seals for you were slain, and by your blood you ransomed people for God from every tribe and language and people and nation, and you have made them a kingdom and priests to our God, and they shall reign on the earth. (5:9–10)

Why is Christ and Christ alone worthy of our trust and worship? Revelation 5:9 tells us, 'for ['because' — Greek *hoti*] you were slain, and by your blood you ransomed people for God from every tribe and language and people and nation'. It is all about atonement, bringing together God and man by sacrifice. In many ways it may strike us as surprising that the resurrection is not mentioned in this passage, although it is certainly implied since John saw a Lamb as if it *'had been'* slain, *standing'* at the centre of the throne. But the emphasis is wholly on the *sufferings* of Jesus. Why? This may well be because, to use the phrase of Bauckham cited earlier, John wants to underline 'the ironic nature of Christ's victorious death'. He conquered through suffering, as even now he is conquering through the suffering of his oppressed people.

Aspects of the atonement

There are three things about Christ's atonement emphasised by this passage.

First, it was a *bloody atonement.* Blood had to be spilt for our wounds to be healed. A price had to be paid for us to be brought back from bondage to sin and the devil. The blood spilt was of infinite worth, the blood of the infinite Son of God himself. All the money in the world could not buy one drop of that blood, for a price cannot be placed upon God's Son. But he has freely given every last drop of that blood so that people from every age and every nationality could be set free from the consequence of sin which is despair on earth now, and misery in hell later.

Secondly, it is a *broad atonement.* People are saved 'from *every* tribe, language, people and nation'. Christ did not die simply for bad people, but for good people, black people, white people, the educated, the illiterate, the cruel, the kind, the sexually pure, the sexually deviant. Whatever social, racial, political or moral group we may care to name, in heaven there will be representatives from them all singing God's praises in heaven.

There is much talk today about the need to be inclusive, but it is *only* the Gospel which offers genuine inclusivity. The inclusion of political correctness is an illusory inclusion for it includes *only* those who subscribe to its authoritarian dogma, the rest are automatically *excluded.* Not so the Gospel of the Lamb. As Charles Wesley put it, 'his blood can make the *foulest* clean, his blood availed for *me.*'

Thirdly, this is a *bountiful atonement.* We are not only freed *from* our sin but freed *for* service (5:10). All believers are priests, representing the world to God in prayer and representing God to the world in proclamation, pleading with people to put down their arms of rebellion and fall into the arms of Jesus. The song repeats the affirmation of 1:6 that Jesus, the Lamb, has made the people to be a *kingdom* and priests, but adds the future promise that they will *reign on the earth*. This fulfils the creation intention that humanity should exercise dominion over the earth (Genesis 1:26) and points to the final victory at the End. The verb 'to reign' is used seven times in this book (5:10; 11:15; 11:17; 19:6; 20:4; 20:6; 22:5) always of God, the Lamb and his followers, anticipating their shared reign in the New Jerusalem. This is the destiny of those who follow the Lamb.

The response to this great achievement is first, the praise of the heavenly court:

> Then I looked, and I heard around the throne and the living creatures and the elders the voice of many angels, numbering myriads of myriads and thousands of thousands, saying with a loud voice, "Worthy is the Lamb who was slain, to receive power and wealth and wisdom and might and honour and glory and blessing!" (5:11–12)

This is followed by the adoration of the entire universe:

> And I heard every creature in heaven and on earth and under the earth and in the sea, and all that is in them, saying, "To him who sits on the throne and to the Lamb be blessing and honour and glory and might forever and ever!" And the four living

creatures said, "Amen!" and the elders fell down and worshipped. (5:13–14)

There are two very important theological points in this passage which are relevant as we think of the Trinity in the Apocalypse.

The first concerns the identity of Jesus. The whole of the Apocalypse is steeped in the monotheism of the Old Testament. As we have seen, Old Testament passages are alluded to and Old Testament language is frequently used.

> One very obvious point must be emphasised; the earliest Christians were *Jews*. Monotheism was the hallmark of Judaism. To be a Jew was to be committed, often fanatically committed, to the maintenance of faith in only one God … For a Jew then, as now, to speak of a man of his own times as divine was as impossible as it is for a Muslim to welcome the Christian doctrine of the Trinity … If one thing was clear and undisputed about Jesus as he lived in Palestine, it was that he was truly human. Yet it was this real man whom his Jewish followers began to regard as divine and ultimately came to call explicitly 'God'.[11]

No creature is to be worshipped, however highly honoured it may be, as John was to discover (22:8–9). Yet here is a creature, the Lamb, who is positioned at the centre of *God's* throne! We have here in symbolic form that which was to be formulated in later Christian theology as the doctrine of the incarnation: in the one person, Jesus, the divine and human natures are united. He is both fully God and truly man.

The praise of the Lamb in chapter 5, which uses the same worship language of God as we find in chapter 4, may constitute the high point of the early Christians' conception of the divinity of Jesus. Having surveyed the evidence that in the early post-Easter period, Christians were learning to think and speak of Jesus in much the same way as they thought and spoke about God, R.T. France notes:

> ... the natural culmination of this process in the last book of the New Testament, where not only is Jesus ('the Lamb') regularly associated with God in his glory and sovereignty (e.g. Revelation 7:14–17; 11:15; 12:10; 14:1,4; 20:6; 21:22f.; 22:1–4), but worship and praise are offered to him equally with the Father (Revelation 1:5f; 5:8–14; 7:9–12; 22:3). The great doxologies of Revelation are not a new experiment involving the worship of one previously regarded in a less exalted light, but the proper expression of attitude to Jesus which has been there from the beginning, increasing no doubt in intensity and in sophistication, but deriving from the impression made by Jesus himself during his earthly ministry.[12]

It is not simply the case that the worship of Jesus indicates that he is divine, but that *because* he is divine he rightly elicits worship.

There is also a polemical aspect to the worship of

Jesus, especially in chapter 5, which would have meant a great deal to John's readers subject to the enticements of imperial Rome.

Rome was set on making maximum impact to secure loyalty from all its citizens, including those living in Asia Minor. One way was to induce a sense of *awe* towards its emperors:

> The colossal statue of Domitian (Titus?) in Ephesus, the presence of cult statues and temples throughout Asia, the impressive processions and other rites involving those cult sites and simulacra [image], replete with choral associations singing hymns to the emperors and gods, all sought to excite awe among the residents of the seven cities (and beyond) contributing thus to the popular legitimation of imperial rule.[13]

There was an additional element to this seduction of the people, which was to attempt to evoke a sense of *gratitude* to the emperors. Gratitude (*charis*) was the response expected to expressions of favour or kindness. Aristotle discussed this in terms of how one could curry the favour of a benefactor and how one should respond to a benefactor in gratitude. 'The cult of *Roma et Augusti* was first and foremost an expression of gratitude towards Augustus and his successors.'[14]

John's vision in chapters 4 and 5 subverts that kind of propaganda, hopefully steeling the Christians to resist it, by enabling them to see it as an outrageous sham, incapable of even beginning to emulate the genuine

'Kingly' worship directed solely to God and the Lamb in the palace of heaven. Prostration before statues of the emperor and singing of hymns of adoration were all part of the grist for the imperial cult, and very impressive it was too (which is what they were designed to be). But there is no comparison to the adoration and hymnology of heaven.

Furthermore, while the emperor might present himself as a great benefactor, this was *not* the reality.

> The first hymn (Revelation 4:11) asserts God deserves public acknowledgement (glory), honour, and power *because* (*hoti*) God created all that is … The second hymn (Revelation 5:9–10) proclaims the Lamb worthy to take the book and open its seals (that is to exercise judgement over earthly kingdoms and usher in God's kingdom) *because* (*hoti*) the Lamb redeemed a people for God to constitute that kingdom by giving up his own life on their behalf, dramatically depicted in terms of being slain and giving his blood as the ransom, fulfilling at last the promise of the creation of a priestly kingdom.[15]

Both lessons need to be learnt by Christians today.

It is only too possible for Christians to be in awe of the glamour and the glitz of modern society, projected into our lives in a thousand and one different ways. We are easily impressed with the impressive. The next step in the seduction is to seek such things for ourselves, so that *we* must appear impressive and successful, and the same goes for our churches. If 'pop idols' (and the term 'idol' is suggestive) draw a large audience, the same formula has been adopted by churches with the result that much of what passes as worship is little more than entertainment. What occurs in some churches is an imitation (and often not a good one at that) of what the world is offering, in a way not dissimilar to that offered by ancient Rome. Both are light years away from the worship of heaven which local churches should be reflecting. The result is, as A.W. Tozer observed decades ago, that 'the Christian conception of God current in these middle years of the twentieth century is so decadent as to be utterly beneath the dignity of the Most High God and actually to constitute for professed believers something amounting to a moral calamity.'[16] One can only hazard a guess of what he would say of Christians living in the twenty-first century! The vision of Revelation 4 and 5 is meant to kindle within us not only a desire for the Most High God, but a grateful submission to him.

This leads us to the second lesson of where we are to direct our gratitude. We observed earlier that one of the effects of secularisation is to produce within us disenchantment; we no longer see the world as a gift to be received with gratitude, but a given which leaves us nonchalant. If we are to be grateful to anyone, we are led to believe it is to the politicians who grant us liberty and prosperity, or scientists and technicians who enable us to retreat into the 'me world' of our games and social networks. If any 'salvation' is to be spoken of, from the disasters of climate change or whatever is the latest spectre, then it is something *we* are to achieve ourselves. The vision of Revelation 4 and 5 counters such foolishness. All that we have, including our scientific abilities, ultimately comes from God and he is to be rendered thanks accordingly. The Father is the great benefactor in creation: in him 'all things were created and have their being' and the Son is the great benefactor in salvation: with his blood he has purchased a kingdom of priests for God to serve the world under God. This means that for the Christian especially, the words of W.B. Auden are to be constantly before them, 'Let all your thinks be thanks.'

The second theological point relates to the mission of Jesus. Even in heaven *the cross is central*. The Lamb looks as if it had been slain. In other words, in heaven Jesus bears the scars of his passion. These indicate his 'intercession' (Greek *entunchano* — 'being around on our behalf,' Hebrews 7:25) for his people as High Priest.[17] The marks of his atonement are for ever before the Father guaranteeing our acceptance and our ability to enter the divine throne room without fear. The marks are visible, however, not for the sake of the Father, but for the sake of his people, assuring them of the sufficiency of his atonement on their behalf: *this* is how they were cleansed. Consequently, all attempts to save ourselves are not only foolhardy but obnoxious. This was well put by C.H. Spurgeon:

> Self-righteousness exclaims, "I will not be saved in God's way; I will make a new road to heaven; I will not bow before God's grace; I will not accept the atonement

which God has wrought out in the person of Jesus; I will be my own redeemer; I will enter heaven by my own strength, and glorify my own merits." The Lord is very wroth against self-righteousness. I do not know of anything against which His fury burneth more than against this, because this touches Him in a very tender point, it insults the glory and honour of His Son Jesus Christ.

The angels and saints in heaven know this is his glory and so break out in the praise of 5:12, they can do no other — and neither can we.

Chapters 4 and 5 give struggling, tempted, enduring Christians a taste of reality, the reality of the triune God who reigns. It is a vision of God which is meant to instil within us awe and draw from us gratitude. Most of all it is meant to create endless devotion. Commenting on these chapters Jonathan Edwards said:

> Christ in the gospel revelation appears as clothed with love, as being as it were on a throne of mercy and grace, a seat of love encompassed about with pleasant beams of love. Love is the light and glory which are about the throne on which God sits ... the light and glory with which God appears surrounded in the gospel is especially the glory of his love and covenant grace.[19]

James Torrance draws together well the person and mighty purposes of Christ, given to us in chapter 5 in John's apocalyptic vision, when he writes:

> The good news is that God comes to us in Jesus to

stand in for us and bring to fulfilment his purposes of worship and communion. Jesus comes to be the priest of creation to do for us, men and women, what we failed to do, to offer to the Father the worship and the praise we failed to offer, to glorify God by the life of perfect love and obedience, to be the one true servant of the Lord. In him and through him we are renewed by the Spirit in the image of God and in the worship of God in a life of shared communion. Jesus comes as our brother to be our great high priest, to carry on his loving heart the joys, the sorrows, the prayers, the conflicts of his creatures, to reconcile all things to God, and to intercede for all nations as our eternal mediator and advocate. He comes to stand in for us in the presence of the Father, when in our failure and bewilderment we do not know how to pray as we ought to, or forget to pray altogether. By his Spirit he helps us in our infirmities.[18]

We worship the Lion who *is* the Lamb.

5. God the Spirit of Revelation

MAX LUCADO TELLS THE STORY OF WHAT ONCE HAPPENED to him as he was taking a flight across the United States:

> The flight attendant told us to take our seats because of
> impending turbulence. It was a rowdy flight, and folks
> weren't quick to respond; so she warned us again. "The
> flight is about to get bumpy. For your own safety, take
> your seats." Most did. But a few didn't, so she changed
> her tone, "Ladies and gentlemen, for your own good,
> take your seats." I thought everyone was seated. But
> apparently I was wrong, for the next voice we heard was
> that of the pilot. "This is Captain Brown," he advised.
> "People have gotten hurt by going to the bathroom
> instead of staying in their seats. Let's be very clear about
> our responsibilities. My job is to get you through the
> storm. Your job is to do what I say. Now sit down and
> buckle up!"[1]

It will come of no surprise to hear that is exactly what they did! What is the moral of that story? It is this: a good pilot will do whatever it takes to get his passengers safely home.

We might similarly ask: How is *God* going to make sure he is going to fulfil his responsibility, if we may put it like that, of getting his people home safely to heaven? How will he ensure they will make it through all the turbulent storms of life which invariably come their way; the storms of persecution, the icy blast of illness, the diseases of doubt and distress?

From what we have had the privilege of seeing so far, as we have glimpsed the throne room which lies at the heart of the universe, we might be excused for thinking that God is rather distant and remote. After all, God is presented as the One who occupies the throne and so making his dwelling place in heaven, not on earth (chapter 4). Jesus the Lamb is certainly victorious through his death on the cross, but he now shares his Father's throne in glory (chapter 5). If God is in heaven and we are on earth how does he connect with us, how is he to make his presence known and the fruits of his victory shared? Or, to put it another way, how will God 'pilot' his people to the safety of their destination of the world to come as they live in the here and now?

This is where the third person of the Godhead comes in: the Holy Spirit. The Holy Spirit has been described as the 'go-between God'.[2] This term brings together his identity as God, and his ministry, 'go-between', forwarding God's purposes in the world who reigns from heaven, not least in the mission of the Gospel.

In the glory and splendour of eternity the Father, Son and Holy Spirit, equal in divinity, supreme in majesty, reign over all. So the blessings which come from the divine throne to God's people having a threefold source: 'Grace and peace to you from him who is, and who was, and who is to come, *and* from the seven spirits *before* his throne, *and* from Jesus Christ' (1:4–5, NIV). Ian Paul observes, 'The insertion of the *seven spirits* between references to God and Jesus makes it impossible to understand it as anything other than a symbolic description of the Spirit as the third person of the Trinity.'3

By speaking of the Holy Spirit being *before* the throne suggests that he too rightly belongs on the divine side of the created order. But there is also a certain 'distancing' from the throne; he is 'before' it, like a royal servant poised to do the bidding of the King. He is the 'go-between God' who links heaven and earth, God and man.

In the Apocalypse we have a distinctive way of referring to the Holy Spirit, that of 'the seven Spirits' or 'sevenfold Spirit'. It would appear that this imagery is drawn from the Greek translation of Isaiah 11. The Septuagint (LXX) speaks of the Messiah being full of the Holy Spirit: 'And the Spirit of God shall rest upon him, the spirit of wisdom and understanding, the spirit of counsel and strength, the spirit of knowledge and godliness shall fill him; the spirit of the fear of God.' According to Beale the passage in

Isaiah 'shows that God's sevenfold Spirit is what equips the Messiah to establish his end-time reign'.[4] It is also part of the paraphrased allusion to Zechariah 4:2–10. In that passage the prophet sees a golden lamp-stand with seven lamps which are the 'eyes of [Yahweh] which range through the whole earth'. As we shall see, there is a further allusion to Zechariah 4 and the lamp-stands in chapter 11.

The reference to the '*seven* Spirits' also needs to be considered against the background of the use of numbers in Revelation, especially the number seven. The book itself is structured by two organizations of seven. In chapters 2–3 there are seven letters to seven churches. In chapters 4–22:5 there are seven visions of the shift of the ages.[5] Together with its multiples, seven is a number which signifies fullness or completion, thus referring to the seven Spirits before God's throne stressing his fullness and totality: 'The sevenfoldness of the Spirit binds his identity to God and to Christ and symbolises both the diversity of his gifts and their unrestricted scope.'[6]

There is another symbol associated with the Spirit in 4:5: 'From the throne came flashes of lightning, and rumblings and peals of thunder, and before the throne were burning seven torches of fire, which are the seven spirits of God.' This is yet another allusion to Zechariah 4 in which the lamp-stands symbolise Yahweh's presence with his people and a new temple built by God's Spirit.[7] In addition to this the '*lampades*' of 4:5 may be another way of referring to the *lychnoi*, the burning torches denoting God's presence as in Genesis 15:17 and Ezekiel's heavenly vision:

> As for the likeness of the living creatures, their appearance was like burning coals of fire, like the appearance of torches moving to and fro among the living creatures. And the fire was bright, and out of the fire went forth lightning. (Ezekiel 1:13)

When connected to the 'lightning' and 'thunder' around the heavenly throne, we are again drawn to the idea of a theophany as at Sinai. The seven Spirits mediate the divine presence.

The number four is also significant, it is the number of the world, similar to the way we speak of the 'four corners of the earth'. The seven Spirits of God is mentioned four times in this book, 1:4; 3:1; 4:5 and 5:3, indicating that *he* is the one who will implement God's will and the victory of the Lamb throughout the entire world. This is of a piece with what Jesus himself taught in John's Gospel. In John 15:26–27 (NIV), Jesus says to his disciples:

> When the Advocate comes [another name for the Holy Spirit], whom *I will send* to you from the Father — the Spirit of truth *who goes out from the Father* — he will testify about me. And you also must testify, for you have been with me from the beginning.

Jesus is about to go back to his Father by way of the cross, and when he returns to heaven as Sovereign — the victorious Lamb — together with his Father he will send his Holy Spirit not only to ensure his presence with his followers on earth, but to enable them to carry out their task of witnessing to him in the world. This is sometimes referred to as the 'executorial authority' of the Spirit.[8] Here the Holy Spirit is understood to act on behalf of Christ in the world (like an executor of a will) while retaining divine authority associated with his divine Personhood (he has authority in his own right as God; think of the case of Ananias and Sapphira who lied *to the Holy Spirit* and were judged accordingly).

Let's now turn and see how all of this is worked out in the Apocalypse.

The sevenfold Spirit communicates the revelation of God

The apostle John is in exile on the isle of Patmos, far removed from the presence of the ascended Christ who is bodily in heaven. However, he is somehow caught up to heaven by the Holy Spirit. Four times John says he was carried away 'in the Spirit' and on each occasion it marks a significant turning point in the book (1:10; 4:2; 17:3; 21:10). To speak of being 'in the Spirit' is a way of saying that John is a receiver of *genuine divine revelation*, just like the prophets in the Old Testament (Ezekiel 1:24). Again, this is simply a fulfilment of what Jesus promised: 'When he, the Spirit of truth comes, he will guide you into all truth. He will not speak on his own; he will speak only what he hears, and he will tell you *what is yet to come*' (John 16:12). It is the Holy Spirit who is the giver of revelatory experience.

We have spoken of a 'revelatory experience' deliberately. It can sometimes be unthinkingly assumed that what John relates by the Spirit is a straightforward *description* of what he saw. But there are some things described which don't make literal visual sense, for example, in John's vision of the heavenly throne the rainbow which surrounded it had the 'appearance of an emerald' which, of course, no rainbow has.

However, as Ian Paul rightly notes, John's construction of the book pays a great detail of attention to the *words* being used. He uses key words which are repeated with certain frequencies:

> He careful repeats a phrase but with consistent variation, such as the fourfold 'every tribe and language and people and nation' repeated seven times but never twice in the same way, and similar repetition-with-variation in the seven mentions of the living creatures with the elders. And he re-uses and reworks Old Testament texts and ideas from all over the canon of Scripture. These all point to a text that has been composed with extreme care over some time.[9]

It is not so much the visionary experiences themselves which are of prime importance, but the *words written*. It is these which constitute the revelation given by God as 'the revelation of Jesus Christ' (1:1). It is these *words* which 'are trustworthy and true' (22:6). The warning at the end of the Apocalypse refers to the sanctity of the words, 'I warn everyone who hears the *words* of the prophecy of this book: if anyone adds to them, God will add to him the plagues described in this book, and if anyone takes away from the *words* of the book of this prophecy, God will take away his share in the tree of life and in the holy city, which are described in this book.'

Ian Paul's conclusion is a sound one:

> Did John have a vision (or series of visions)? (The episodic nature of the text suggests that John might have had a series of visions. But the overarching presentation of what John writes offers the whole as a single visionary experience.) If he did, he has reported it in a very careful way. We don't have a vision; we have a vision report, a text, and we should attend to it. John's aim is not to impress us with his visionary experience, nor (necessarily) to encourage us to have our own. Rather, John wants us to order our lives in the light of the truth about God that these vision reports reveal to us.[10]

The sevenfold Spirit communicates the message of Jesus

We see this clearly in the letters to the seven churches. Each letter begins with something like, 'These are the *words* of him who is the first and the last' and conclude with 'whoever has ears let him hear what the *Spirit says* to the churches' — present tense. Sometimes in a church gathering you will hear people who want to introduce some innovative off-the-wall idea with, 'We need to listen to what the Spirit is saying' by which they mean that somehow we have to discern the Spirit's voice outside Scripture. John would tell us that if we *really* want to know what the Spirit is saying, we are to turn to this book because *this* is what the Spirit is saying to us *today*. We are not to create a gap between the words of Jesus recorded in Scripture and the speaking of the Holy Spirit to his people today. The Spirit takes the words of Jesus which are inscripturated and enables the church to understand and apply them. They do not change as he does not change, for he is 'the same yesterday, today and forever' and so is his revelatory message (1 Peter 1:23–25).

It is important that we notice how the main focus throughout is on Jesus *himself*, the Spirit's work being to get God's people to fix their hearts and minds upon *him*. Hence, we have these magnificent, awe inspiring introductions to the churches, 'These are the words of *him* who holds the seven stars in his right hand and walks among the seven golden lampstands'; 'These are the words of *him* who is the First and the Last, who died and came to life again'; 'These are the words of *him* who has a sharp, double-edged sword'; 'These are the words of the So*n of God*, whose eyes are like blazing fire and whose feet are like burnished bronze' (Revelation 2:1, 8, 18, NIV). Jesus had said of the Spirit, 'He will glorify *me* because it is from me that he will receive what he will make *known* to you' (John 16:14, NIV).

This is how C.H. Spurgeon describes this particular Christ-honouring role of the Spirit:

> It is ever the Holy Spirit's work to turn our eyes away from self to Jesus; but Satan's work is just the opposite of this, for he is constantly trying to make us regard ourselves instead of Christ … We shall never find happiness by looking at our prayers, our doings, or our

feelings; it is what *Jesus* is, not what we are, that gives rest to the soul. If we would at once overcome Satan and have peace with God, it must be by 'looking to Jesus'.[11]

The Holy Spirit is like the sun, we are not meant to look directly *at* him, but *by* him look to Jesus and understand everything else in his light. Robert Murray M'Cheyne captures this thought perfectly:

> Learn much of the Lord Jesus. For every look at yourself, take ten looks at Christ. He is altogether lovely. Such infinite majesty, and yet such meekness and grace, and all for sinners, even the chief. Live much in the smiles of God. Bask in His beams. Feel His all-seeing eye settle on you in love, and repose in His mighty arms ... Let your soul be filled with a heart-ravishing sense of the sweetness and excellency of Christ and all that is in Him.[12]

This has a transforming effect. The Spirit changes us by this message in order to become more like the one who is the content and the originator of the message, the Lord Jesus Christ. 'Scripture is both the cradle where the incarnate Christ lies and the sceptre by which the ascended Christ now rules the church.'[13] The exercise of that sceptre of the ascended Christ is very much in evidence in the seven letters, but not only those, the whole of the Apocalypse is in one sense the sceptre extended to God's people everywhere at every time. Its purpose is twofold, to 'inform us about Christ and to form Christ in us'.[14]

The sevenfold Spirit communicates the presence of God

In 5:6 we read:

> And between the throne and the four living creatures
> and among the elders I saw a Lamb standing, as though
> it had been slain, with seven horns and with seven eyes,
> which are the seven spirits of God sent out into all
> the earth.

We have already drawn attention to the meaning of the
horns symbolising strength and power, in this case seven
horns signifying *perfect* power. The eyes denote Jesus'
all-seeing capacity; note again the number seven — his
knowledge is perfect and complete: he discerns all things,
including the thoughts of people's hearts. The question
then arises: how is this perfect power and knowledge of
Jesus in heaven to be communicated on earth? Here we
are given the answer — by the seven Spirits: '*The Lamb*
had seven horns and eyes [referring to Jesus' omnipotence
and omniscience] *which are* the seven spirits of God *sent
out into all the earth.*' It is the Spirit which brings Christ's
strength and wisdom to the world which amounts to him
mediating Christ's presence. This is how the ascended
Christ, who is bodily in heaven, is able to stand amongst
the lamp-stands of the churches in Asia Minor. The Holy
Spirit is the Spirit of *Jesus* (cf. Acts 16:6).

This work of mediating Christ's presence occurs throughout the world

Jesus told his disciples, 'Nevertheless, I tell you the truth:

it is to your advantage that I go away, for if I do not go away, the Helper will not come to you. But if I go, I will send him to you (John 16:7). While he was on earth, in the flesh, Jesus was limited by space and time. He could not be in two places at once. But now, with the sending of the Spirit, everything has changed — there are no barriers of time or space to prevent his followers having an intimate relationship with him, everywhere at every moment. In fact, it is even *more* intimate because while on earth Jesus was *with* his disciples, now by his Spirit he is *in* his disciples. That is what this symbolism signifies.

But you may be thinking, 'Isn't God everywhere anyway? Isn't that part of the definition of God, who he is, that he is *omnipresent?*' That is true, of course. But the way God's presence is experienced and the significance of his presence will vary. We have been given a glimpse of what God's presence is like in heaven in all its breathtaking grandeur. But that doesn't mean he is confined there. As Stephen Charnock wrote, heaven 'is the court of his majestical presence, but not the prison of his essence'.[15]

Sometimes God is described as being 'far'; his presence is not experienced as blessing but as judgement. As Charnock says, 'When he comes to punish, it notes not the approach of his essence, but his strokes of justice.' But God's nearness is something very different: 'When he comes to benefit, it is not by a new access of his essence, but an efflux of his grace.' Charnock concludes:

> He departs from us when he leaves us to the frowns of his justice; he comes to us when he encircles us in the

arms of his mercy; but he was equally present with us in both dispensations, in regard of his essence.[16]

All the seven churches experienced the essence of God by the ministrations of the sevenfold Spirit, but in different ways, for some it was in judgement, for others it was the enfolded 'arms of mercy'.[17]

One of the things which is of concern to the ascended Christ is the spiritual quality of life of the believers in the churches. In Pergamum, sexual immorality is a danger and needs to be repented of (2:14–16), likewise in Thyatira (2:20). Ephesus appears to be theologically sound but lacking in love (2:4). Those in Laodicea are living lives hardly distinguishable from the surrounding pagans. Despite their love feasts Christ stands outside the door of the church knocking to gain entry (3:20)! These are some of the concerns for the local churches, each being an expression of the heavenly, invisible church gathered around the throne of the Lamb (7:9). Christ's desire is for each church to be increasingly conformed to that heavenly church, hence the warnings and encouragements.

In some measure, what is happening around the throne in the heavenly 'catholic' church is meant to be happening in those local churches. It is the sevenfold Spirit, in bringing the message and presence of Christ, who enacts the transformation. In short he beautifies:

> The chief end of life is to glorify God and enjoy him for ever (this is what we see happening in heaven in chapters 4 and 5), and the chief means for doing so is

to achieve a beautiful body. This is the task of the Holy Spirit, who creates and perfects the church, the body of Christ. Primary beauty is best seen in persons who love as God loves. Praising God in song is a vital part of the curriculum of worship, part of the pedagogy of the church as that beauty school that seeks to produce forms of individual and communal holiness.[18]

The all-powerful, all-knowing seven spirits is working this within the local churches of God.

R.A. Torrey unpacks one implication of this truth which should help us when dealing with temptation. He says:

How often some young man has had his hand on the door of some place of sin that he is about to enter and the thought has come to him, 'If I should enter there, my mother might hear of it and it would nearly kill her,' and he has turned his back on that door and gone away to lead a pure life, that he might not grieve his mother. But there is One who is holier than any mother, One who is more sensitive against sin than the purest woman who ever walked the earth, and who loves us as even no mother ever loved. This One dwells in our hearts, if we really are Christians, and he sees every act we do by day or under cover of the night; he hears every word we utter in public or in private; he sees every thought we entertain, he beholds every fancy and imagination that is permitted even a momentary lodging in our mind, and if there is anything unholy, impure, selfish, mean, petty, unkind, harsh, unjust, or any evil act or word or thought or fancy, he is grieved by it.'[19]

There you have it, 'The Lamb had seven horns and seven eyes, which are the seven spirits of God sent out into all the earth.' Thankfully, as well as the eyes — the one *who sees all*, there are the horns — the power, the one *who provides all* so that we are changed by the Spirit to increasingly love what he loves and despise what he despises.

The sevenfold Spirit enables the witness of God

In 1:5 the blessings which come to the churches from the throne of the triune God identify Jesus first and foremost as 'the faithful *witness.*' Given the close connection between Jesus and the Spirit, it would be reasonable to presume that one of the primary roles of the Spirit will be that of witnessing. But who does he facilitate to enable this witnessing to the Gospel? The answer is the churches which are symbolised as golden lamp-stands. In chapter 11 these themes are brought together by an allusion to a prophecy in the Old Testament which we have already mentioned, Zechariah 4. In that vision the prophet saw a golden lamp-stand with seven lamps, together with two olive trees, whom, we are told, are servants of the Lord who will carry out their work, 'Not by might, nor by power but *by my Spirit* says the LORD' (Zechariah 4:6). Without going into all the details, what we have in chapter 11 of Revelation is the declaration that Christians in the local congregations are to be God's witnesses (11:3), standing for God's truth in the face of opposition, just as Elijah and Moses had done in their day (11:6), and Jesus in his day (11:8). And although some will be killed (in Greek, the word for witness is *marturia* from which we get our word martyr), nonetheless, by the breath of God, which is the same as the Spirit of God (11:11), not only will it be as if they had not died because witness to the Gospel goes on in the power of the Spirit, but ultimately they will be raised to life by the Spirit just as he raised Jesus to life after three days in the tomb.

According to Richard Bauckham, witness is one of the main themes of Revelation and is connected to the dominant concern with truth and falsehood:

> The world is a kind of court-room in which the issue of who is the true God is being decided (that was of course the big issue with Elijah on Mount Carmel — who was God). In this judicial contest Jesus and his followers bear witness to the truth. At the conclusion of the contest, their witness is seen to be true and becomes evidence on which judgement is passed against those who have refused to accept its truth: the beast and its worshippers.[20]

This is very much in accord with what Jesus said to his disciples in John's Gospel, 'When the Advocate, whom I will send to you from the Father — the Spirit of truth who goes out from the Father — *he will testify* about me. And *you also must* testify.' The role of the Spirit is to enable Christians to fulfil their role of testifying to the nations by proclaiming the Gospel. Part of the witness is the unstoppability of the Gospel despite persecution.

In AD 178 a Gallic slave girl, Blandina, who was a recent convert to Christ was brought before the local authorities for her faith and said, 'I am a Christian woman, and nothing wicked happens among us.' She was then forced to watch the murder of her Christian friends, then was heated on a gridiron, thrown to the wild dogs and finally impaled on a stake. Totally true to her Christian character she died praying for her persecutors. And you know what? Her death movved a fifteen year old boy, Ponticus, to follow her example. As one of the early church leaders, Tertullian, put it, 'The oftener we are mowed down by you the more we grow in number. The blood of Christians is seed.'[21]

The same happened in Cambodia when, in the 1970s, a third of Cambodia's population were wiped out by the communist Khmer Rouge. Many of those who were killed were murdered because they were Christians. Here is part of an account of one such Christian family, that of Haim:

> Curious villagers watched as the Khmer Rouge ordered the family to dig their own graves. Then, consenting to Haim's request for a moment to prepare themselves for death, father, mother and children, hands linked, knelt together around the gaping pit. With loud cries to God, Haim began exhorting both the Khmer Rouge and all those looking on from afar to repent and believe the gospel. Then in panic, one of Haim's young sons leapt to his feet, bolted into the surrounding bush and

disappeared ... the Khmer Rouge and the stunned family kneeling at the graveside, looked on in awe as Haim began calling his son, pleading with him to return and die together with his family. 'What comparison, my son,' he called out, 'stealing a few more days of life in the wilderness, a fugitive, wretched and alone, to joining your family here momentarily around this grave but soon around the throne of God, free forever in paradise?' After a few tense minutes the bushes parted, and the lad, weeping, walked slowly back to his place with the kneeling family. 'Now we are ready to go,' Haim told the Khmer Rouge. But by this time there was not a soldier standing there who had the heart to raise his hoe to deliver the death blow on the backs of these noble heads. Ultimately this had to be done by the Khmer Rouge communal chief, who had not witnessed these things. But few of those watching doubted that as each of these Christians' bodies toppled silently into the earthen pit which the victims themselves had prepared their souls soared heavenward to a place prepared by their Lord.

But it didn't end there because the writer goes on to say that after the death of Haim and his family,

The rapid news of such as this, of certain Christians boldly bearing witness to their Lord in death, was gossiped about the countryside. Eventually these reports were brought across to the refugee camps in Thailand, and not always by Christians, but by typical

Cambodians who, until then, had despised the *Puok Yesu,* the people of Jesus.[22]

What has become of Jesus' promise of joy to Haim and his family? They are part of the great assembly singing the praise of the Lamb who was slain. It was the sevenfold Spirit who gave life to Blandina and Haim and his family in drawing them to Jesus in faith. It is the same Spirit who gives resurrected life.

What that might look like in heaven, where the work of the sevenfold Spirit is completed in glorification, is imaginatively described by Jonathan Edwards as he expands an image originally conceived by William Tyndale that, 'Where the Spirit is, there it is always summer':

> All shall stand about the God of glory, the fountain of love, as it were opening their bosoms to be filled with those effusions of love which are poured forth from thence, as the flowers on earth in a pleasant spring day open their bosoms to the sun to be filled with warmth and light, and to flourish in beauty and fragrancy by his rays. Every saint is as a flower in the garden of God, and holy love is the fragrance and sweet odour which they shall send forth, and with which they fill paradise.[23]

What a vision — what a Saviour!

6. The Anti-Trinity of Revelation

REVELATION 13 IS DOMINATED BY MONSTERS: THE BEAST rising from the sea, the creature coming out of the earth and the dragon which stands behind them both. Just in case anyone is tempted to smile condescendingly at this, dismissing it as belonging to a more primitive and mythical age, it might be worth pausing to ask why is it that monsters figure so prominently in all cultures throughout the world and down the ages, including our own? Could it be that deep down we are profoundly conscious that there is such a thing as *evil*, but we can't see it?

Jeffrey Dahmer was a serial killer, submerging himself in cannibalism and necrophilia. He looked like the boy from next door, sweet and polite. The Milwaukee jury who tried him concluded that he wasn't insane, he was just plain evil. Peter and Amy Grossberg appeared to be an ordinary upper-middle-class college couple in New Jersey. They delivered a child in a motel room, then caved in its head and dumped it in a skip. What they did was evil. We look for visible signs of evil on the faces or in the eyes of people who do such things but don't see any; they seem to be, well, just like us. It is baffling that evil can reside within a person without leaving a visible mark. So perhaps because we know that evil is real, and we expect to see realities, that we give it form in our imaginations in order for us to see some shape of it in the real world.[1] In other words, monsters are a way of saying evil is real, evil is terrible and evil is dangerous. Monsters have distorted features because evil distorts, monsters are strong because evil has power, monsters fly because evil is as quick as a flash of temper. Monsters may not actually exist, but the evil they represent certainly does.

In the Old Testament Book of Job we are presented with two monsters, the Behemoth and Leviathan (Job 40–41). The Behemoth is the plural form of a common Hebrew word simply meaning 'beast'. So in Job we might have 'the Beast' *par excellence*. The Leviathan is sometimes referred to as 'Rahab' which has a whole army of cohorts (Job 9:13), it is the 'gliding serpent'. The Leviathan is the ultimate sea monster, lurking in the dark depths of the sea; full of destructive power but not beyond the sovereign, constraining control of Yahweh (Psalm 74:13–14).[2] Both ideas of the beast and the serpent are replete with meaning and are relevant to the imagery of Revelation 13.

The Old Testament uses the imagery of monsters for a very significant reason, not because they exist but because *what* they depict exists. In the Bible monsters signify creation gone wrong, chaos reigning, God's good world spoiled. Sometimes they represent nations in their aggression and idolatry.³ At other times they stand for satanic powers and the ultimate conflict that will lead to the new heavens and the new earth. In biblical thinking it is not a matter of light versus darkness in the abstract but God versus evil powers in personal form.

In the Apocalypse John takes some of these traditional materials regarding monsters, including the references to multiple heads and horns, to depict not only the Roman Empire of his day but the growth of other world powers throughout history, until Christ comes when he shall finally judge and abolish all evil. John the seer points beyond the *human* instruments to the *demonic* powers that manipulate them.

We will take a look at each of the three creatures in turn. The fact that there are *three* of them is highly significant, as we shall see.

The dragon by the shore

'The dragon stood on the shore of the sea' (13:1). We have already been given the identity of the dragon in verse 9 of the previous chapter:

> The great dragon was hurled down — that *ancient serpent* called the *devil,* or *Satan,* who leads the whole

world astray. He was hurled to the earth, and his angels with him. (12:9, NIV)

De Silva points out that John doesn't have to work hard to demonstrate the enmity of the dragon towards God and his people, because it would be readily accepted as such within both a Jewish and Christian culture.[4] However, John does describe the dragon's activity as a basic reminder of the fact. We see this in chapter 12 by the depiction of the dragon's aggression towards the male child (12:4) identified as the Christ by the use of Psalm 2:7,9 (12:5–6); his warring against the heavenly hosts of God (12:7–9); his identification as the historic enemy of humankind (the 'serpent', 12:9), the deceiver and accuser ('Satan') of the whole world and the enemy of the church depicted as the woman in the wilderness and her offspring (12:12).

Whilst there is no second god, for the Bible disavows any absolute dualism, there is a supernatural creature operating behind the scenes. He has the title 'the Satan', which means 'challenger'.[5] He is also called the devil, meaning the one who makes false accusations. This is a creature which lies, corrupts, loves the stench of death and will use whatever means at its disposal to take forward its programme of destruction. Little wonder that monster imagery is used to depict it!

However, although the dragon is portrayed as darkly malevolent, chapters 12 and 13 are to be considered against the backdrop of the previous chapters, not least the reign of the creation-redeeming Trinity of chapters 4 and 5. In his book, *The Serpent of Paradise*, Erwin Lutzer writes:

> The devil is just as much God's servant in his rebellion as he was in the days of his sweet obedience ... We can't quote Luther too often: The devil is God's devil. Satan has different roles to play, depending on God's counsel and purpose. He is pressed into service to do God's will in the world; he must do the bidding of the Almighty. We must bear in mind that he does have frightful powers, but knowing that those can only be exercised under God's direction and pleasure gives us hope. Satan is simply not free to wreak havoc on people at will.[6]

This is a very important truth to be borne in mind as the chapter unfolds.

At the beginning of chapter 13 the dragon is standing on the shore of the sea poised to engage in something sinister. The question is: what? In the previous chapter we were told that the dragon had been waging war on Christians, 'those who keep the commandments of God and hold to the testimony of Jesus' (12:17). Now he is about to further ratchet up the aggression by summoning from the sea a beast of such immense power that the peoples of the world are overawed by its stature and intimidated by its strength. Little wonder that they exclaim, 'Who is like the beast? Who can wage war against it?' (13:4, NIV).

The beast from the sea (13:1–10)

The origin of the beast being from the sea is significant. As we saw when we considered the sea of glass before the throne in Revelation 4, the sea symbolised chaos and rebellion for the Jews.[7] And so it is legitimate to surmise that this is a creature who will exhibit all the traits of the place of its origin, in wreaking havoc and railing against the order of the Creator.

Whatever this beast is it has great strength. It has the speed of a leopard; the might of a bear and inspires the terror of a lion (13:2). These are all echoes of Daniel 7:1–8, 19–21. It has tremendous authority too, for it has a throne and wears ten crowns on its horns and has seven heads (13:1). Furthermore, it has been through many battles, having at one point received what appeared to be a fatal wound (13:3,12) but within a short time it has soon recovered and is back displaying greater ferocity and prowess than before and so appears unbeatable. This is what happened with ancient Rome. After one Cæsar died, he was replaced with another and then another, until we come to Domitian at the time of John and the reign of terror begins all over again.

Not only does the beast display overwhelming power, appearing invincible, but it sees itself as answerable to no one, least of all God, for it acts as if *it* were God, 'uttering blasphemies' and demanding allegiance and worship, which belong to God alone (13:5–6). What is being presented by this imagery is a world power; the whole world is astonished by it, standing in awe of its greatness (13:3). Its might is formidable and its influence irresistible as every people group comes under its sway according to 13:7, 'authority was given it over every tribe and people and language and nation'.

If you were living in the first century and this passage

was read to you, you would pick up on the symbolism straight away: this is imperial Rome. Here is the arrogance of the Cæsars who took to themselves divine titles. In the 60s the Emperor Nero had coins minted on which he was referred to as 'the Saviour of the World'. In the 90s, which was probably when this book was written, the Emperor Domitian insisted people address him as, 'Our Lord and our God.' What is being described in the first instance, is the gruesome reality of the only Empire to have lasted a thousand years, the Roman Empire: 'The use of the word "beast" indicates that the Roman Empire was not humane; it was not a kingdom that cared for its citizens and existed for their benefit. Instead, it was like a carnivorous animal, rapacious and cruel, ripping open and consuming all those who opposed it.'[8]

People go along with this authority not simply because they are coerced, but deceived; they fall for the lie that this kind of government has divine qualities. John deliberately has the beast parodying the Lord Jesus. The worshipful response of the people in verse 4, 'Who is like the beast?' is stolen from the worship of Yahweh in the Old Testament: 'Who is like you among the gods, Lord? Who is like you, glorified among the holy ones?' (Exodus 15:11 LXX). The beast with its seven heads and ten horns takes on the image of the dragon and receives the dragon's throne and authority. This runs parallel to Jesus receiving all power and authority from the Father and being seated on his throne (2:27). According to 13:3, the beast had a head (leader) who was literally 'slain unto death' which mimics John's description of a Lamb standing as though slain (5:6). The beast is then said to have 'lived' (*ezēsen*) after being mortally wounded (13:14) which parodies Jesus' resurrection in 1:18, 'I died and behold I am alive for evermore.' Also, having seen the beast restored to life, the whole earth worships the beast and the dragon, aping the heavenly praise which 'every creature' gives to God and the Lamb in 5:13. The beast is both like and unlike Christ. This is a cheap, but effectively deceptive, imitation. John is using parody to raise awareness amongst Christians of the counterfeit to which they are being subject almost on a daily basis. As Greg Carey observes, 'John uses parody to unmask imperial *hubris* … Parody is especially appropriate where appearances are deceptive; it is the perfect tool for revealing imperial pretensions.'[9] What we have in Revelation 13 is 'the Unholy Scam'![10]

What a dangerous world

The dark, brooding scenario which the Book of Revelation paints is that a world in rebellion is a world without hope. The attempt to remove and replace God, to declare him to be in effect dead, results in a world which is frightening, brutal and dangerous.

The attempt to kill off God, as it were, and render belief in God as something evil or at least irrelevant, has been gathering momentum since the middle of the nineteenth century, mainly through the work of the German philosopher, Friedrich Nietzsche. He was the self-proclaimed 'immoralist', 'anti-Christ', and 'conqueror of God'. He wrote a parable in which the main character,

Zarathustra, was the first person to use the phrase 'God is dead', meaning that he never really existed and the sooner we wake up to the fact the better. In the story, Zarathustra says to a young man (a believer), 'There is nothing of what you speak; there is no devil and no hell. Your soul will be dead even sooner than your body, so don't fear anything anymore.' That is, religion in general and Christianity in particular is fantasy. Nietzsche claimed that man was like a rope, stretched between an animal and a Superman. This is his evolutionary position and we need to hasten on to the next stage: the super-race. This is achieved by what he called 'the will to power'. You would not be surprised to discover that many of these ideas were taken up and applied with great fervour by Adolf Hitler.

Power in power

One thing which stands out above all else in this apocalyptic nightmare is the dominance and abuse of power, hence the reference to thrones and crowns. It is by the exercise of power that the nations are subdued. It is people and political systems, which in abandoning God become agents of a supernatural evil power, taking on the features of ferocious animals like leopards, bears and lions. When God is banished from his world, at least in thought, then literally all hell breaks loose sooner or later. In such circumstances there is no clear way of deciding what is right or wrong. Consequently might *is* right. If there is no God to whom men and women are accountable and no external frame of reference for morality, an ethical pole star by which to navigate, then it is dog eat dog and so you had better make sure you are the bigger dog!

Think for a moment of what is being exposed concerning the depth and extent of sexual abuse in the UK and USA, both in society and the church, which has been going on for years. At root it is the abuse of *power*. Some politicians, media personalities, gangs of men, even priests, all have power over the weak and the vulnerable and feel they, like the beast, are accountable to no one. What is more, they have been colluded with by those whose duty it was to protect such people. That is the dragon at work for sure. Worst still is when such corruption and abuse becomes *institutionalised* and the State wields its power to suppress truth and the Christian religion because it cannot brook any rivals. This is happening in Muslim countries all around the world, in North Korea, in China and increasingly in the West. Whether it is Islam, Marxism or any other ideology, they all have the appearance of something unnaturally powerful. Little wonder that the world cries out, 'Who is like the beast?'

The beast from the land (13:11–18)

With the first beast the emphasis is on *power*, with the second beast the stress is on *deception*. The second beast has many of the characteristics and goals of the first, because both beasts are different aspects of the same entity: totalitarian powers which insist on directing the spiritual and physical lives of those under their control. Oppressive powers often need deception to reach their goals and fulfil their programmes. Hitler had his Goebbels who claimed 'We do not talk to say something but to obtain a certain effect', and spoke of 'the Big Lie'.

This 'other beast' is spoken of as 'coming out of the *earth*', rather than the sea, as a way of showing the spread of this evil through the human population. He *looks* like a lamb but *speaks* like a dragon — he has the appearance of a benevolent, even a religious force, but his so called 'truth' is a lie. His words lead to the worship of evil disguised as good, which is the first beast who in turn is a 'front' for the dragon. Here the focus moves from power to propaganda. In a parody of true religion the second beast represents *false religion*. He has all the paraphernalia of the religious practitioner including the ability to perform signs and wonders (13:14). Consequently he will dazzle and impress his audience. His mission is to turn the inhabitants of earth into the *willing* worshippers of the first beast and behind that, the great dragon — Satan. The dragon continues the same work today. Sometimes it is blatant and unmistakable.

Gary Haugen was in Kibuye, Rwanda in 1994 shortly after the massacre, directing the United Nations genocide investigation. Kibuye had suffered from two horrendous slaughters, one in the cathedral and the other in the local stadium. On the one hand, Haugen later wrote, 'it was a filthy, stinking job, but it had to be done'. On the other hand, what undid him were not the nameless, faceless, decaying body parts but the painful glimpses of the uniqueness of each victim expressed in such objects clutched in death as wedding pictures and Bibles with loving inscriptions. He wrote:

> For as difficult as it was to imagine, each crumpled mortal frame had indeed come from a mother, one single mother who somewhere in time had wept tears of joy and aspiration over her precious child.

That experience never left him. Determined to make a difference he founded the International Justice Mission (IJM) to stand up to the abuse of power and provide advocacy and rescue for the oppressed of the world, who have no champion to speak for them. Of the diverse forms of brutality and oppression all grow from the same source, according to IJM, namely, abuse of power. This, in turn, relies on two tactics: coercion (force) and deception (lies). There is always some attempt to compel the weak to do something they don't want to do, sometimes using brute force, but sometimes employing more subtle means like threatening to withhold financial aid. There is also deception, perhaps covering actions with legal justification, or acting in the name of 'religion', weaving a web of lies and deceit, until eventually no one knows what the truth is anymore or who is to blame. The result is that often the perpetrators get off scot-free. IJM seeks to expose this.[11]

Sometimes it is more subtle and hardly noticed until it is too late. Such is the new totalitarianism which is at work in the West. It masks itself as being concerned with inclusivity and tolerance, but if challenged it immediately excludes and is brutally intolerant. The ideology is cultural Marxism; the cutting edge of what has become a culture war is alleged LGBQT+ rights.[12] Remember that we are dealing with deception, with Satan's aim of destroying that which is God-given and good. Occasionally the beast makes a slip and lets the cat out of the proverbial bag. This happened with the Lesbian author and activist Masha Gessen when she said:

> Fighting for gay marriage generally involves *lying* about what we're going to do with marriage when we get there. Because we lie that the institution of marriage is not going to change, and that is a *lie.* The institution of marriage is going to change and it should change, and again, *I don't think it should exist.*[13]

The beasts in the West

Let's think how Revelation 13 is working itself out today in the West involving the use of the power of the State, the effective communication of false ideologies, and the co-operation of organised religion. First, there is the interference of the State in education which seeks to normalise same-sex relations.

Here is one example. The 'No Outsiders' teaching training resource by Andrew Moffat, which taught and promoted same-sex relationships, was used in his own Parkfield Community School, a primary school in Birmingham together with five other schools. This school has a 98% Muslim intake. This led to massive protests by parents outside the schools and withholding their children from attending. The parents were labelled 'homophobic extremists' with the teachers being portrayed as the victims who simply wanted to get on with their job of educating the children. The then Minister for Schools, Nick Gibb, in a letter to *The Times* wrote:

> The protests outside a primary school in Birmingham which teaches the fact that same-sex relationships are normal and are as loving and supportive as any heterosexual relationship are in my view wrong. I support the city council's decision to secure an injunction against those protests taking place near the school. It is bizarre and horrific that we allow protesters outside primary schools with placards to target those who teach what is legal and wholly appropriate in today's society.[14]

Notice what he says. He speaks of teaching '*the fact* that same-sex relationships are normal' and that this is 'wholly *appropriate* in today's society' and objects to parents exercising their right to protest.

In some schools, lobby groups are being brought in, not in order to educate but indoctrinate, for example the 'Mermaids' movement on transgender, and 'Educate and Celebrate' on LGBTQ, and 'Drag Queen Story Time' readings in primary schools involving transvestites. These are means of grooming our future citizens while they are most susceptible. Elly Barnes of 'Educate and Celebrate' is quite candid about the primary aim of the organisation which is 'to completely smash heteronormativity ... that is what we want to do so our kids can grow up to be who they are.'[15] This is, of course, wholly disingenuous for they don't want 'kids to grow up to be who they are' (which would on the whole be normal heterosexuals) but rather mess them up in order to provide a greater pool from which homosexuals can fish.

When there is religious sanction for anti-God ideology, even when made with good intentions, the new cultural totalitarianism is almost complete, which is what we are increasingly seeing happen in the Church of England, it becoming the religious mouthpiece for the progressive agenda.[16]

If one does not go along with the prevailing ideology which is given religious backing, life soon becomes intolerable:

> Also it causes all, both small and great, both rich and poor, both free and slave, to be marked on the right hand or the forehead, so that no one can buy or sell unless he has the mark, that is, the name of the beast or the number of its name. (13:16)

There may be economic sanctions. But punitive restrictions can be imposed in other areas too: the right of free speech and the right for parents to decide what's best for their children. Such prohibitions will be made in the name of high-sounding principles such as inclusivity, tolerance and equality, but the actions taken betray the deception for what it is by producing opposite results. Rather than having a liberal society, illiberality becomes the order of the day.

To summarise, what we see in Revelation 13 is an '*anti-Trinity*' — a grotesque parody of the genuine thing. Christ received authority from the Father (Matthew 11:27; 12:16ff), so the first beast, the Antichrist, receives authority from the dragon (13:4). As the Holy Spirit glorifies Christ (John 16:14), so the second beast, the false prophet, glorifies the Antichrist (13:12).

The number of the beast

What are we to make of 13:18: 'This calls for wisdom: let the one who has understanding calculate the number of the beast, for it is the number of a man, and his number is 666'?

There are several things which can be said with a fair degree of certainty.

First, we are told that it is 'the number of a man'. The word *anthropos* need not refer to a specific individual, it could be equivalent to 'humanity'.

Secondly, we have already noted the significance of the number '7' which is the number of completion, thus '666' symbolises a falling short, an inadequacy of some kind.

Thirdly, in recent years the significance of triangular numbers in the ancient world and in Scripture has been highlighted.[17] This is the sum of successive integers (1+2+3+4 etc.). The number 666 is the thirty-sixth triangular number. In Revelation square numbers are used to represent the things and people of God, this triangular number represents opposition to God.[18]

Does the symbol have any specific reference for John and his readers? Ian Paul convincingly argues that there is:

1. We are told that the 'number' is a 'name' and is to be worked out.

2. The practice of gematria whereby the numerical value of names was calculated by adding up the value of individual letters was widespread. Both Hebrew and Greek letters were assigned numerical values and there is evidence of the use of this device in the New Testament, for example, the prologue to John's Gospel consists of 496 syllables and the epilogue 496 words in Greek. 496 is the numerical value for 'only begotten' (μονογενὴς).

3. The term 'beast' (Greek *therion*) which is a transliteration of the Hebrew (TRYWN) comes to 666 (400+200+10+6+50). Interestingly enough, so does the name Nero (Greek *Neron*), transliterated into Hebrew (NRWN QSR: 50+200+6+50+100+60+200=666).[19]

This being a reference to Nero would certainly fit both historically and theologically. But this does not mean that the symbolism is restricted to him because both here and in 17:9 there is a call for 'insight' and 'wisdom', namely, for God's people to 'see through' the claims of imperial Rome. For all its displays of power backed up by religious ceremonial and pretensions of bringing 'peace' to the world, it is in reality nothing of the sort. Nero is representative of the idolatrous tyranny characteristic of

Rome and all other authorities who would defy God and his Christ and take to themselves divine-like prerogatives. God's people today require no less wisdom and insight to identify the 'power idols' of their time.

All of this seems like bad news for the world and Christians in it. Is there any good news to be found? Indeed there is. Being Trinitarian we will consider three items of good news.

First, God is in control even when it looks as if he isn't. In 13:7 we are told that the first beast was 'given' or 'allowed' (*edothe*) power to wage war on the saints and to have authority over all people. Who allowed this? The answer: God! His enemies can go so far but no further. Even when Christians are persecuted and people follow false ideas, it is only because of divine permission. Therefore, there is hope because God is still sovereign. Luther's comment mentioned earlier is worth reiterating, 'If there is a devil, he is God's devil.'

> Twenty-one times in Revelation we read the words 'it was given' (*edothe*), and in every instance God is the one who does the giving. God is unblemished by evil, and his motivations are not evil, as opposed to those of the dragon and the two beasts. And yet the dragon and the beasts are not outside the realm of God's sovereignty.[20]

Secondly, not everyone worships the beast. The ones who surrender to the anti-God powers are those whose names have '*not* been written in the Lamb's book of life, the Lamb who was slain from the creation of the world' (13:8, NIV). The implication is that those for whom Christ died, whose divine love was fixed upon them in eternity past, will be taken into eternity future because their names *are* written in his book. They can be reassured he won't abandon them: how could he when he has died for them?

Thirdly, in the light of this knowledge of God's sovereign saving love for his people Christians are called to 'patient endurance' and be 'faithfulness' (13:10, NIV).[21] What might such patient endurance look like?

In his book entitled, *Passion*, Karl Olsen tells the story of such endurance among the early French Protestants called Huguenots:

> In the mid-18th century in … southern France, a girl named Marie Durant was brought before the authorities, charged with the Huguenot heresy. She was fifteen years old, bright, attractive, marriageable. She was asked to abjure [renounce] the Huguenot faith. She was not asked to commit an immoral act, to become a criminal, or even to change the day-to-day quality of her behaviour. She was only asked to say, 'J'abjure'. No more, no less. She did not comply. Together with thirty other Huguenot women she was put into a tower by the sea … for thirty-eight years she continued … And instead of the hated word 'J'abjure' she, together with her fellow martyrs, scratched on the wall of the prison tower the single word 'Resistez', resist!' … The word is still seen and gaped at by tourists on the stone wall … We do not understand the terrifying simplicity of a

religious commitment which asks nothing of time and gets nothing from time. We can understand a religion which enhances time ... But we cannot understand a faith which is not nourished by the temporal hope that tomorrow things will be better. To sit in a prison room with thirty others and to see the day change into night and summer into autumn, to feel the slow systemic changes within one's flesh: the drying and wrinkling of the skin, the loss of muscle tone, the stiffening of the joints, the slow stupefaction of the senses — to feel all of this and still to persevere sees almost idiotic to a generation which has no capacity to wait and endure.[22]

Every new generation is called to wait and endure by the One who has conquered (13:10).

7. The Victory of the Trinity

THE YEAR 1989 HAS BEEN WIDELY DESCRIBED AS THE 'YEAR of the century'.[1] With the collapse of the Soviet Empire, a surge of optimism swept around the world. The images which stuck in the minds of many were the scenes in Wenceslas Square in Prague, where night after night a quarter of a million people were stirred by the mesmerising speeches delivered by the slim, boyish, moustached figure of the then dissident but later President, Vaclav Havel. As speaker after speaker drew the contrast between themselves, the revolutionaries and the totalitarian regime, the Czech crowd broke out into a chant: 'We are not like them!' The 'them' being the Soviet regime described as 'People of lies and propaganda'. The 'we' were the revolutionaries describing themselves as 'people of truth'. The motto of the Charter 77 Movement of which Havel was a leading member was 'Truth prevails for those who live in truth.'

At the time it seemed that Soviet tanks were going to be far more persuasive than calls for truth. But we all know what happened. The whole system came falling down like the unstable house of cards it was.

The same claim had been staked out by the one man dissident movement, Aleksandr Solzhenitsyn, who, in his Nobel Prize speech declared, 'One word of truth outweighs the entire world.'

Of course, standing for truth invariably means a price has to be paid. Truth, like grace, is never cheap. Both Solzhenitsyn and Havel suffered imprisonment. Truth, however, cannot be imprisoned. Certainly attempts will be made to suppress it or distort it, but no matter how intensely such purges of truth occur, reality will win out in the end. In the words of Jesus, 'The truth shall set you free.' It is the victory of Truth, or to be more precise, the victory of the triune God who is Truth, which moves towards a climax in chapter 19 of the Book of Revelation.

So far we have seen the first two stages of the victory of the triune God — a victory that was carried out by the Son, at the behest of the Father 'who is, and who was and who is to come', applied by the sevenfold Spirit.

Stage one is the faithful witness of the death of the Passover Lamb who initiates a new Exodus by way of his sacrifice on the cross. It was there that Satan, the deceiver, and death itself had been effectively defeated. We see this especially in chapters 5 and 12.

Stage two is the creation of a people drawn from the

nations who have purified themselves by the blood of the Lamb. These have been formed into a kingdom of priests by Christ (chapters 1 and 5). It is by their witness to the truth in Christ in the power of the Holy Spirit, that people are set free and the kingdom extends over the earth (chapter 11). For some this will be a witness made all the more glorious and effective in martyrdom as they are opposed by the beast and the false prophet and, ultimately, Satan, who stands behind them (chapters 12 and 13).[2]

The third and final stage of the victory of the Lamb is when he returns to consummate his kingdom, deliver his judgement and abolish evil. This is encapsulated in part in chapter 19.

The triumph of the faithful

I saw heaven opened, and behold, a white horse! The one sitting on it is called Faithful and True, and in righteousness he judges and makes war. His eyes are like a flame of fire, and on his head are many diadems, and he has a name written that no one knows but himself. He is clothed in a robe dipped in blood, and the name by which he is called is The Word of God. And the armies of heaven, arrayed in fine linen, white and pure, were following him on white horses. From his mouth comes a sharp sword with which to strike down the nations, and he will rule them with a rod of iron. He will tread the winepress of the fury of the wrath of God the Almighty. On his robe and on his thigh he has a name written, King of kings and Lord of lords. (19: 11–16)

This marks the beginning of a new section for John, echoing the earlier new beginning in 4:1, 'I saw a door open in heaven.' But there is a significant difference, heaven *itself* is opened and rather than John being caught up *to* heaven, a figure comes down *from* heaven. We are told that this heavenly figure rides a white horse, white being the symbol of victory, but also a stallion that would have been considered befitting a ruler. We are then given the identity of this figure; he is the one who is 'Faithful and True'. We know this to be Jesus because of a similar title found in 3:14, where he is described as 'the faithful and true witness'. However, in the present vision the idea of 'witness' has been dropped. Why? It is possibly because during his time on earth, and through the work of the Spirit through his people, Jesus bore testimony to the truth of God as Creator and Redeemer in order that people might repent and be saved. But now the time of witness is over because the end of time has come and it is too late. Instead of coming as Saviour, he comes as Judge, to judge people according to the truth; he 'judges *and* makes war' (19:11). To speak of 'judge' in this way means he will do 'what is right' which is why the ESV adds 'in righteousness.' By adding 'makes war' we are being reminded that this is not a single event, but a continuous action he has been engaged in. Although war imagery is used, it is modified by judicial imagery; judging and so subduing and defeating God's enemies: 'This is not the slaughtered Lamb turned slaughterer, but it is the witness turned judge.'³

As we saw in Revelation 13, Satan leads the world astray through lies. Jesus, 'the Word of God', judges the world in truth. The sword he slays with comes from his mouth which means it is a *word* of judgement (19:15). His eyes are like blazing fire (19:12) that is, he is a divine judge who sees infallibly, burning away all false pretence and hypocrisy, exposing the true thoughts of our hearts. He wears many crowns, a symbol of his status; this is the superlative king, which is literally spelt out on his robe at thigh height, 'King of kings and Lord of lords' (19:16). The word for 'crowns' is *diadema,* a symbol of his power to rule, whereas the previous word, *stephanos,* 'wreath' speaks of victory (4:10). It is because Jesus is victorious that he has been given the right to rule, consummating the reign of God.

To know someone's name (especially that of a deity or demon), was in the culture of the time considered to signify possession of power over that person. Accordingly, the rider has a name which is known to him *alone.* This is a way of saying that Jesus can't be overpowered by anyone or anything. He is the supreme ruler. Furthermore, he is now revealed for all the world to see as the promised Messiah of Psalm 2, who will rule the nations with an 'iron sceptre' and will execute God's wrath which is why his robe appears to be dipped in blood (19:13).

The vision is related in the *present tense.* This means that although it lies in the future, Christ's second coming is *so* certain that it can be written down as taking place *now*.

Those who make up Christ's army in 19:14 are the saints, who also ride white horses and are dressed in white, clean linen, symbols of victory and purity. But what is so unusual about this army is that it doesn't actually *do* anything. This is because Jesus has done and will do it all. He is the one who saves and he is the one who judges and so this army doesn't have to engage in combat; it is simply in attendance to watch Jesus put the world to rights and right all wrongs.

The necessity of judgement

Why is it important that it is Jesus who judges and the saints are the ones who watch?

Throughout the Bible God promises future judgement. In the Book of Revelation, organised anti-God human rebellion is spoken of as 'Babylon', the great Prostitute (e.g. 18:9–24). When it is embodied in the form of governmental powers it is 'the beast'. These powers flout God's laws in immorality and shed the blood of Christians in persecution, in 18:24: 'And in her was found the blood of prophets and of saints, and of all who have been slain on earth.' When this aggression takes place, as it does in many parts of the world today, how are Christians meant to respond? We have already seen in earlier chapters that they are called to persevere, remain faithful and witness in love. The natural inclination, however, will be to become bitter and seek vengeance. That is not to be the case.

The way of the early Christians was modelled by a twenty-two year old African girl, Perpetua, in AD 203. With a baby at her breast she was martyred for her faith in Carthage. Her father had tried everything to make her renounce her faith. First, he was rough with her, but found that had no effect. Then he turned to appeals; his grey hairs, her mother and her own tiny son who would not survive without her. All of these were thrown into the scales to induce her to change her mind and deny Christ. But she followed the way of her Saviour. Very quietly, and with great dignity and courage, she went to her death.[4]

However, this does not mean that the longed-for justice will not eventually be seen. It will be by the Lord Jesus who alone is eminently qualified to judge. He cannot be accused of acting capriciously, in a fit of rage, for he has exercised great patience and restraint as through his people he has been reaching out to a rebellious world with the Gospel. He alone, from all the people in the world, has been perfectly faithful and true to God the Father; accordingly the Father hands over to him the divine prerogative to judge. This ensures that justice will be carried out on all those who have inflicted such pain and misery in the world, and have appeared to have got away with it:

> Witness to the truth is double-edged. On the one hand, it is the only means of willing people from lies and illusion to the truth. So it can convert people from the worship of the beast to the worship of the one true God. But, on the other hand, witness which is rejected

becomes evidence against those who reject it. Those who love lies and cling to delusion in the face of truth can only be condemned by truth.[5]

Although it may seem strange to us living in the West, with our weakened concept of justice which is now almost entirely construed as restorative rather than retributive, we are told at the beginning of chapter 19 that the saints will actually *rejoice* when this judgement takes place:

> After this I heard what seemed to be the loud voice of a great multitude in heaven, crying out, "Hallelujah! Salvation and glory and power belong to our God, for his judgments are true and just; for he has judged the great prostitute who corrupted the earth with her immorality, and has avenged on her the blood of his servants." (19:1–2)

Over two hundred and fifty years ago, the American theologian, Jonathan Edwards, commenting on this passage struck the right note:

> Indeed [the saints] are not called upon to rejoice in having their revenge glutted, but in seeing justice executed, and in seeing the love and tenderness of God towards them, manifested in his severity towards their enemies.[6]

God so loves his children that, like with any caring parent, his anger is aroused when bad things happen to them. Jesus said the same, 'But whoever causes one of these little ones who believe in me to sin, it would be better for him to have a great millstone fastened around his neck and to be drowned in the depth of the sea' (Matthew 18:6). What we are seeing here is that anger which has been delayed in time eventually breaking out at the end of time, and God's people will see that he really does love them and is concerned with justice, bringing the two together in the final judgement.

The fate of God's foes

> Then I saw an angel standing in the sun, and with a loud voice he called to all the birds that fly directly overhead, "Come, gather for the great supper of God, to eat the flesh of kings, the flesh of captains, the flesh of mighty men, the flesh of horses and their riders, and the flesh of all men, both free and slave, both small and great." (19:17–18)

Whereas the previous section focused on Christ, here the emphasis is on the fate of those who reject him. The great angelic messenger irradiates such brightness that even though he is standing in the sun he outshines it, indicating it is an angel of great importance. And indeed he is, for he makes a pronouncement regarding the 'great supper of God'.

The scene is of the aftermath of a battlefield with the vultures circling overhead. They are the ones addressed by the angel and called upon to effectively gorge themselves on what is left lying around on the ground after the judgement of Christ has taken place, as we see in the next vision in 19:21. This scene is a variation on another prophecy in the Bible:

> As for you, son of man, thus says the Lord God: Speak to the birds of every sort and to all beasts of the field: "Assemble and come, gather from all around to the sacrificial feast that I am preparing for you, a great sacrificial feast on the mountains of Israel, and you shall eat flesh and drink blood. You shall eat the flesh of the mighty, and drink the blood of the princes of the earth — of rams, of lambs, and of he-goats, of bulls, all of them fat beasts of Bashan. And you shall eat fat till you are filled, and drink blood till you are drunk, at the sacrificial feast that I am preparing for you. And you shall be filled at my table with horses and charioteers, with mighty men and all kinds of warriors," declares the Lord God. (Ezekiel 39:17–20)

What John's vision depicts is the total and final defeat of all those who oppose God. This is universal in scope: '*all men*': free and slave, great and small. Social status and prestige will mean nothing on that day. The only thing that will matter will be whose side people are on — God's or the Satan's — there is no neutrality.

It might be worth saying a word or two about the objections raised against this kind of imagery.

Robert Royalty considers such 'eschatological threats' as an attempt by John to 'bully the churches into accepting his views'.[7] It was visions like these in the Apocalypse which provoked the ire of D.H. Lawrence condemning

John's 'betrayal' of the New Testament's vision of love with his 'lake of burning brimstone in which devils, demons, beasts and bad men should frizzle and suffer for ever and ever, Amen!'[8]

John, however, is not out of line with the teaching of the rest of the Bible, and, indeed, with that of Jesus himself. We have already seen how this vision is a variation on a theme in Ezekiel. This prophet had no difficulty in holding together God's kindness and justice, as we find in Ezekiel 11:20 when God says, 'they may walk in my statutes and keep my rules and obey them. And they shall be my people, and I will be their God'. This is immediately followed by the solemn declaration, 'But as for those whose heart goes after their detestable things and their abominations, I will bring their deeds upon their own heads, declares the LORD GOD' (11:21).

What are we to make of D.H. Lawrence's claim that John is betraying the New Testament's vision of love? If this is the case then the same charge must be levelled at Jesus himself, a point well made by D.A. Carson:

Jesus is the one who introduces the most horrendous and colourful images. He can openly say to those of his followers who are at risk of being crucified and beaten and sawn apart and the rest: 'Do not be afraid of those who kill the body but cannot kill the soul. Rather, be afraid of the One who can destroy both body and soul in hell' (Matthew 10:28). He talks about dungeons and chains and outer darkness ... Jesus speaks of wailing and gnashing of teeth ... So if people think that warning people of hell is manipulative, they must charge Jesus with manipulation.[9]

Similarly de Silva writes:

> Above all, John's presentation of a God who holds rebellious humanity accountable for their affronts against God's honour and rightful claim to obedience resonates with the sayings of Jesus. Matthew 13:41–43 is a case in point: 'The Son of Man will send his angels, and they will gather together out of his kingdom all the stumbling blocks and those practising unlawfulness and will throw them into a fiery furnace; weeping and gnashing of teeth shall be there. Then the righteous will shine like the sun in the kingdom of their Father. Let the one having ears to hear listen.' John in the apocalypse is defining more precisely what constitutes 'the stumbling blocks' and 'unlawfulness' in his own pastoral situation.[10]

The folly of God's enemies

> And I saw the beast and the kings of the earth with their armies gathered to make war against him who was sitting on the horse and against his army. And the beast was captured, and with it the false prophet who in its presence had done the signs by which he deceived those who had received the mark of the beast and those who worshipped its image. These two were thrown alive into the lake of fire that burns with sulphur. And the rest were slain by the sword that came from the mouth of

him who was sitting on the horse, and all the birds were gorged with their flesh. (19:19–21)

We are still dealing with the same scene, the final battle, but the focus has switched to the fate of the beast and its false prophet. The beast represents a state-enforced attempt to overthrow God and his ways, and the prophet is the aid of false religion which can appear as an ideology. We see this, for example, in communism. There is the false prophet (Marx), false Bible (*Das Kapital*), false doctrine (dialectical materialism), false apostles (Lenin, Stalin, Mao), and false hope (the arrival of a communist utopia). But there are other variants of the same theme throughout history.

The irony is that so confident are the God-opposing forces, that they decide to go for an all-out assault on Christ and his followers (19:19). This is the same misplaced confidence that General Custer demonstrated when he rode into Little Big Horn with his seven hundred troops, only to be confronted by 2,500 Sioux and other warriors. The result: total annihilation!

What is strange, however, is that there is *no final battle* as such. We simply have it recorded that, 'the beast was captured and with it the false prophet'. This is almost an anti-climax. It's like watching a film of D-Day and the allied invasion of Europe on the 6 June, 1944 with 8,000 aircraft flying overhead and 7,000 ships crossing the channel. But instead of showing the landing on the beaches, the film suddenly cuts to allied troops entering Berlin! You might well feel cheated. But John is making an important point by presenting it in this way. In the Greek John uses what is called 'the divine passive' to convey the fact that it is all of *God's* doing. Without wishing to sound irreverent, the victory is so easy that God doesn't even break into a sweat. For all the deception, the enslavement of people's minds, the ruining of lives and, in many cases, the annihilation of countless millions through wars and mass killings in concentration camps and the like, those responsible are themselves destroyed in the most frightening way imaginable, 'The two of them were thrown alive into the fiery lake of burning sulphur.' It is abrupt and as jolting as that. 'Alive' speaks of conscious torment and 'burning with sulphur' adds stench to the pain. To be sure these are metaphors being used — picture language — but that doesn't lessen the seriousness of what is being portrayed, rather it heightens it. Even metaphors are incapable of depicting the seriousness of judgement: they fall short because the reality is going to be far, far worse. As for those referred to simply as the 'rest', presumably they are those who have followed anti-god ideologies and so too will be judged by Christ by 'the sword coming out of his mouth'.

In our present world, lies and deceit, bullying and coercing, seem to have the upper hand. The Orwellian nightmare of 'doublethink', as we see for example with the pressure to admit more than two genders, when, as a matter of biological fact, there is male and female, is very much *our* world — the world of the beast and false prophet. But on that Last Day no such blurring or twisting of the truth will be possible, when faced with the

God of truth. There will be no arguing with him because, to many people's everlasting shame, the truth which they had for so long denied and derided will be present for all to see in person, and there will be no escaping him. Solzhenitsyn will be shown to have been right, 'One word of truth outweighs the entire world.'

Making a decision

The final victorious conclusion of the war is not in doubt, but what often is in doubt is on which side men and women are to be found. We are surrounded by people who are effectively good pagans; decent, nice, everyday folk whose lives would not be much different if all religion disappeared from the earth tomorrow. To them God may be a reasonable possibility but never a ruling reality. Perhaps they want God on the sidelines, but never at the centre. Jesus Christ may be admirable, but he is optional, expendable, and certainly not 'King of kings and Lord of lords' (19:16). We may have grown used to this situation, but according to the Apocalypse, the triune God has not. The whole Book of Revelation is an exposure and a protest against it. The imagery is gruesome, and deliberately so, because the rebellion against the glory and kindness of God is so great that the judgement of God, which will eventually come, must match it. The question the book leaves its readers with is: 'Which side are *you* on?'

8. The Trinity in Heaven

IN THE FINAL BOOK OF HIS CLASSIC, *THE CHRONICLES OF Narnia* entitled *The Last Battle*, C.S. Lewis has the Pevensie children, together with their cousin Eustace, trying to take in the new creation. As they do so they find themselves discussing how much it is like and unlike Aslan's country:

> 'If you ask me,' said Edmund, 'it's like somewhere in the Narnian world' ... 'I don't think *those* ones are so very like anything in Narnia,' said Lucy. 'But look there ... Those hills ... the nice woody ones and the blue ones behind — aren't they very like the Southern border of Narnia?' 'Like!' cried Edmund after a moment's silence. 'Why they're exactly like' ... 'And yet they're not like,' said Lucy. 'They're different. They have more colours on them and they look further away than I remembered and they're more ... more ... oh, I don't know ...' 'More like the real thing,' said the Lord Digby softly.[1]

Who knows, maybe we will be having conversations like that when we enter the new heavens and earth. There will be much which will be familiar to us but, I suspect much, much more which will be different. Perhaps the colours will be more vivid and more numerous; the perfume of the flowers more delicate and more lasting. We really don't know, but Lewis is surely right when he says through the character of the Lord Digby that it will be '*more* real'. Because of the limitations of our imagination, we tend to think of the future life as a kind of shadowy existence, less substantial than this one, when in fact it will be the exact reverse. How can we be sure this will be so? Because of the imagery in the final chapters of the Book of Revelation where we see that the triune God is 'all in all'.

What we are being presented with is not so much a picture of Paradise regained, as Paradise surpassed. There are certainly echoes of Eden with mention of a river (Genesis 2:10), trees providing fruit for food (Genesis 2:9), the tree of life (Genesis 2:9), the idea of worshipping or serving God by taking care of the garden in Eden, whereby Adam is presented as a kingly priest (Genesis 2:15). There is the close, intimate nature of the relationship between God and man (Genesis 2:7), as well as the devastating fall-out of sin resulting in God's curse, banishment from the garden and a barring of re-entry by the placing of a fiery angel across its entrance (Genesis 3:23–24). But as we shall see, in the new world not only are the effects of the curse undone and reversed, but, 'all that the original garden could have been is expanded and intensified'.[2]

In chapter 21 this new world is seen as a city which descends from heaven:

> Then I saw a new heaven and a new earth, for the first heaven and the first earth had passed away, and the sea was no more. And I saw the holy city, new Jerusalem, coming down out of heaven from God, prepared as a bride adorned for her husband. (21:1–2)

This reminds us that Utopia is not a human achievement which we can work up, but a gift of God which comes down. It also points us to the truth that our place in the new world will involve us being in a perfect community, using our ever-developing gifts, talents and energy in carrying on God's great creation project. We are told in 21:22 that there is no temple in this City as God *himself* is the temple. This means in everything we carry out there will be worship; everywhere we go we will be with God, and all we do will be priestly as well as kingly. Indeed, this is what we were created and redeemed for, to reflect back perfectly God's image, which is the image of Jesus, *the* priestly King. John Piper describes it in this way:

> Being loved by God is the exhilarating deliverance from the hall of mirrors we once thought would bring us happiness — if we could just like what we see. Heaven is not a hall of mirrors. Or maybe we should say, heaven is a world in which all created things have become mirrors, and all of them are tilted to a 45 degree angle. Everywhere we look — in every creature — we see the reflection of God.[3]

The picture of heaven and the new world as a city is highly suggestive as Jonathan Edwards reminds us:

> Heaven is likened in Scripture to a splendid and glorious city. Many men are surprised and amazed by the sight of a splendid city. We need not be told how often it is called the holy city of God. Other cities are built by men, but this city, we are told, was built immediately by God himself. His hands reared up the stately mansions of this city, and his wisdom contrived them. Hebrews 11:10, 'For he looked for a city which has foundations, whose builder and maker is God.' Other cities that are royal cities, that is, cities that are the seats of kings and where they keep their courts, are commonly, above all others, stately and beautiful; but heaven, we are told is the royal city of God, where the King in heaven and earth dwells, and displays his glory. Hebrews 12:22, 'The city of the living God.'[4]

In chapter 22 we move from the city to the garden, or rather we discover it to be a *garden city*.[5] The ancient world commonly had gardens surrounding temples; indeed, the term 'paradise' was the Persian word for garden. So maybe the vision being given to John is that the approach to the city is by way of a garden, or perhaps it is a city patterned with gardens. Whatever it is, we are not to lose sight of the fact that this is not a tourist guide of the new creation, a kind of 'Google map heaven' — it's the *symbolism* that matters. Let's explore some of these word pictures to whet our appetites for what is to come to all those who are followers of the victorious Lamb.

All blessings come from God

It is surely no mere coincidence that Genesis 3 ends with the way back to Eden blocked by an angel (Genesis 3:24), while John is introduced to the new Eden by an angel, 'Then the *angel* showed me ...' (22:1). What is shown to the seer is a river. One of the remarkable things about this river is that it doesn't flow *beside* the city or even *into* the city and then out again as you would normally get with ancient cities, for example Babylon. Instead, it wells up from *within* the city itself, ensuring a continual source coming from the throne of God and the Lamb.

As we saw in chapters 4 and 5 of the Apocalypse, the throne of God lies at the centre of the universe in the old creation; here it is to be found at the centre of the new universe, occupied by the same rulers, God (the Father) and the Lamb (God the Son). We also see in 22:3 that the throne of God and the Lamb (plural) will be in the city and his servants will worship *him* (singular). What flows from the throne are the 'waters of life' which in John's Gospel are associated with the outpouring of the Holy Spirit (John 7:38 also see Ezekiel 47). Once again we encounter the one true God in all his triune, life-giving majesty: Father, Son and Holy Spirit. This is the Trinity of the new earth which has been touched by heaven. It is a breathtaking picture which is meant to be savoured by believers.

The imagery of the river sparkling like crystal presumably reflects the light of God's glory, mentioned back in 21:23. It flows in all its sweet purity down the middle of the city's main street. This is in stark contrast to what would normally have coursed down the streets of many Roman cities, which were open sewers! This water is clean, pure and refreshing, accessible to *all* the inhabitants of the new world.

Just as the tree of life was planted in the middle of the Garden of Eden (Genesis 2:9–10), John sees the tree of life growing on each side of the river (22:2). We are not to become side-tracked by such questions as: 'How can a tree be on both sides of a river at once?' We are meant to have a *literate* reading of Revelation, not a *literal* reading. We are dealing with apocalyptic literature which works with ambiguity, paradox and contradictions. The thought we are to grasp is that the tree of life is accessible to *everyone* no matter which side of the river they may be on; the Spirit touches *all*. This might also be linked to the idea that it is the Spirit who gives life, as rivers give life to trees which grow beside them. Both symbols merge, to underscore the truth that those who are in the new creation are given eternal life by the Spirit. That life is maintained by eating of the tree of life which is freely and constantly available, hence twelve crops of the same fruit every month of the year.

After the rebellion in the Garden, Adam and Eve tried to hide their shame by covering themselves with fig leaves (Genesis 3:7); the leaves of the tree of life act like a poultice which heals the nations. One of the terrible effects of the Fall was the introduction of enmity and suspicion amongst people (Genesis 3:13–15), eventually issuing in wars and conflict (Genesis 4:8–12). But there will be no such things in the new world for, according to 22:3, there will be no curse.

The overall picture is of a world from which there is a complete absence of all the negative associations of our present existence — 'night will be no more' (22:5). This is significant because for the ancients, night-time was a dangerous period; this was when wild animals would prowl, enemies would attack and thieves break in under the cover of darkness. But there will be no darkness in the new age, indicating that God's people will be completely secure, having the illumination of God's own presence: 'They will need no light of lamp or sun, for the Lord God will be their light, and they will reign forever and ever' (22:5). There are some places in our major cities where it would not be wise to venture out at night, but no such restrictions will be in force in God's new and perfect world. There will be no fear, no anxiety, no 'what ifs' — just complete peace and security.

All glory goes to God

What makes heaven, *heaven*? What makes the new creation really *new*? Is it that there is no pain? Or that it is a place where we will be reunited with those we love who have died in the faith, such that all will be well in 'the sweet by and by'? Whilst not denying any of those things, surely what makes heaven *heaven*, and the new creation *new*, is that *God* is there and we have unlimited access to him.[6] Heaven would not be heaven without Jesus;

life without him is hell. At the present time we walk by faith, loving Jesus whom we can't see (1 Peter 1:8–9), but there we shall *always* have him before us, he will never be hidden from our sight: 'No longer will there be anything accursed, but the throne of God and of the Lamb will be in it, and his servants will worship him. They will see his face, and his name will be on their foreheads.' (22:3–4)

The beauty of the Lord

One of the great blessings pronounced by the priests to the people in the Old Testament is found in the Book of Numbers 6:25–27: '[Yahweh] make his face shine on you and be gracious to you; [Yahweh] turn his face toward you and give you peace' (NIV). In the new world order, that blessing will be fully realised. The Psalmist prays, 'One thing I ask from the LORD, this only do I seek: that I may dwell in the house of the LORD all the days of my life, *to gaze on the beauty of the LORD* and to seek him in his temple' (Psalm 27:4, NIV). In eternity that prayer will be answered in full. If you are a Christian one day you will *see,* with transformed new eyes, God in the face of Christ; his beauty will so transfix your gaze and delight your heart that in one sense you won't be able to take your eyes off him for a single heavenly second.

Service of the Lord

But as we look upon him, we shall also serve him (22:3). Although in the Book of Revelation Christians are described as resting 'from their labours' (14:13), this doesn't mean that they will be idle in the new age. Believers, we are told, will *serve*, which is a worship word (*latreusousin*). Just as Adam was created to work in the garden and to do so joyfully, so shall we in this garden. Our work will not be the toil Adam experienced after the curse, for there will be no curse (22:3). In the age to come we will be able to use our renewed human powers at full stretch, getting stronger, not weaker with every activity, exploring and developing this new world of perfect love in perfect power.

A world of joy and love

Sometimes people deride and dismiss the notion of heaven as 'boring'. George Bernard Shaw put into words what many people think:

> Heaven as conventionally conceived is a place so inane, so dull, so useless, so miserable that nobody would venture to describe a whole day in heaven, though plenty of people have described a day at the seaside.[7]

Similarly, writer Laurie Lee declared that Heaven was:

> Too chaste, too disinfected, too much on its best behaviour, it received little more than a dutiful nod from the faithful. Hell, on the other hand, was always a good crowd-raiser, having ninety percent of the action — high colours, high temperatures, intricate devilries, and always the most interesting company available.[8]

The philosopher, A.J. Conyers also notes the disappearance of heaven from the popular mind:

> We live in a world no longer under heaven. At least
> in most people's minds and imaginations that vision
> of reality has become little more than a caricature,
> conjuring up the saints and angels of baroque frescoes.
> And in the church only a hint remains of the power it
> once exercised in the hearts of believers.[9]

The picture of saints sitting around on clouds strumming harps all day long draped in a celestial negligée has captured the collective imagination. However, it is a dreadful caricature and travesty of the truth.

In some of his parables Jesus more than hints that those who have served him faithfully on earth will be given greater responsibilities and joys of serving him in heaven (Matthew 25:14ff). This is one reason why it is so important not to be a 'couch potato' Christian, because depending upon what we sow on earth so will our reward be in heaven. Put starkly and simply: don't do much for Jesus now and you won't be doing much for him then either. But we might well ask: why would we not want to be about our Master's business, one who is as glorious and splendid as this? We should be all out and out for him — he is such a kind King who offers us as a gracious gift a complete, sin-free universe.

J.C. Ryle preached a sermon entitled, 'Christ is All' which is relevant at this point:

> But alas, how little fit for heaven are many who talk
> of "going to heaven" when they die, while they have
> manifestly no saving faith, and no real acquaintance

> with Christ. You give Christ no honour here. You have no communion with him. You do not love him. Alas! What could you do in heaven? It would be no place for you. Its joys would be no joys for you. Its happiness would be a happiness into which you could not enter. Its employments would be a weariness and burden to your heart. Oh, repent and change before it is too late.[10]

In order to enjoy the new heaven and the earth as it is meant to be enjoyed, beholding the beauty of Christ, right habits need to be cultivated in the present. This is what should be happening each time the church meets, the local congregation itself being a 'projection' of the heavenly 'catholic' church which is before the throne of the Lamb ('catholic' comes from two Greek words, *kata* — according to, *holos* — whole).

> After this I looked, and there before me was a great multitude that no one could count, from every nation, tribe, people and language, standing before the throne and before the Lamb' (7:9, NIV).

The worship of Christians gathered together by the Gospel on a Sunday should be both *anticipatory of* heaven and *preparatory for* heaven. This is where Christ is, moving amongst the lamp-stands by his Spirit, and this is where he is to be adored and obeyed, as he is perfectly worshipped bodily in heaven. There needs to be a recapturing of what the church *is* and what the church is *for* amongst Christians. Kevin Vanhoozer describes this renewed vision:

We must no longer think of the church as an antechamber to heaven, a place to wait around. Rather, the church — the company of those in union with Christ — is an anticipation of heaven, a place to begin practising it, because Christ is among us. It is a local embassy of God's kingdom, a parable of the kingdom of heaven localised on earth.[11]

Furthermore, serving involves *reigning*, 'And they will reign for ever and ever' (22:5). Adam with his wife Eve failed in their commission to reign over the world under God and for God, by allowing sin to reign over them instead. They were not found worthy to do that which God called them, and us, to do. But now there is one who is worthy, as we saw in chapter 5, the Lamb, who has made his followers a 'kingdom' (5:5). In 11:15 we are told that Christ 'shall reign for ever and ever'; here in chapter 22 the exact phrase is used but this time of his people. We shall reign, because Christ reigns and we shall reign with him and will be able to do so because we will be made like him, bearing the image of the one who *is* the image of the invisible God (Colossians 1:15). We shall be given new bodies fit for a new heaven and earth enabling us to serve him and each other in perfect love without any impediment.

There is a new day coming

There is going to come a day when the whole of the universe is going to be radically transformed (Romans 8:19–23), and we are going to need transformed bodies to inhabit it. Our physical ears of this age will need to be attuned to the sweet music of the next age. We will need new eyes to see the new colours of whatever sunsets there may be in the next world; new fingers to feel the new sensations of a world untainted by sin; new vocal chords which will carry the praises of God in a new atmosphere so that everything is worthy of the triune God. In short, our bodies will be like the glorious body of Christ, together with our hearts and minds (1 Corinthians 15:50–58). Try and imagine how wonderful it will be to wake up each day in that glorious new world and our first thought in the morning will be of God, and not how much our back aches! Won't it be a sheer delight to hear not birds singing, but angels, whose delicious sound of adoration and joy will make even the finest rendering of Bach's 'Jesu Joy of Man's Desiring' sound as if it were being played on a beginner's recorder in comparison? Jesus is glorious, and the astonishing thing is that we will be glorious too, and find in him complete satisfaction:

> How blessed therefore are they that do see God, that are come to this exhaustless fountain! They have obtained that delight that gives full satisfaction; being come to this pleasure, they neither do nor can desire more. They can sit down fully contented, and take up with this enjoyment for ever and ever, and desire no change. After they have had the pleasures of beholding the face of God millions of ages, it won't grow a dull story; the relish of this delight will be as exquisite as ever. There is enough still for the utmost employment of every faculty.[12]

All heaven is of God

One of the most captivating descriptions of the new heaven and earth in the last two chapters of the Book of Revelation, is how God's radiant presence touches everything, everywhere; 'And the city has no need of sun or moon to shine on it, for the glory of God gives it light, and its lamp is the Lamb' (21:23).

God's glory is not something separate from God himself, any more than the rays of the sun are separate from the sun. God's being *is* glorious, shining out to enlighten and bestow life — his 'communicative, spreading goodness' to use the phrase of Richard Sibbes.

As the sun gives light and heat, God's glory is in the giving of himself in the Lord Jesus Christ by the Holy Spirit ('We have seen his glory, the glory of the one and only Son, who came from the Father, full of grace and truth' John 1:14, NIV). 'The beautiful glory of the triune God is radiating, self-giving love.'[13]

The *person* of Christ is the lamp which shines, illuminating everything and everyone. Similarly in chapter 22, the Lord gives light; the throne is in the *middle* of the *city*, in contrast to the early chapters of Revelation, where it is in *heaven* out of sight from mere mortals. But not in the new age, when God will be everywhere such that no corner of his universe escapes his stunning, love effusing, triune presence.

Perhaps no one has described this anticipated reality

that all heaven is of God, its source and goal, better than Jonathan Edwards:

> God is the inheritance of the saints; he is the portion of their souls. God is their wealth and treasure, their food, their life, their dwelling place, their ornament and diadem, and their everlasting honour and glory. They have none in heaven but God; he is the great good which the redeemed are received to at death, and which they are to rise to at the end of the world. The Lord God, he is the light of the heavenly Jerusalem, and is the 'river of the water of life' that runs, and the tree of life that grows 'in the midst of the paradise of God'. The glorious excellencies and the beauty of God will be what will forever entertain the minds of the saints, and the love of God will be their everlasting feast. The redeemed will indeed enjoy other things; they will enjoy the angels, and will enjoy one another: but that which they enjoy in the angels, or each other, or anything else whatsoever, that will yield them delight and happiness, will be what will be seen of God in them.[14]

The big picture as Apocalypse

In a way, what is condensed in apocalyptic language in the Book of Revelation is a biblical theology of the Bible. From creation to new creation, Adam, the head of humanity to Jesus the head of a new humanity, banishment from Eden to Eden surpassed: all woven together into a rich tapestry of imagery which is intended to strengthen faith, and inspire hope in the God who is Father, Son and Holy Spirit.

In his inspiring study, *The King in His Beauty*, Thomas Schreiner rightfully states that Revelation is a fitting conclusion to the canon of Scripture:

> God is the sovereign king over all, according to Revelation. Even when evil seems to reign, God rules over the events of history. Believers may entrust their lives to him, for judgement is surely coming for those who resist his will. The future kingdom that is promised to the patriarchs and the prophets and to the psalmists will surely come. The prayer that God's kingdom to come and for his will to be done will be answered. The new heaven and new earth are coming. The land of promise of the OT is dialled up to include the whole universe, and the whole universe is portrayed as God's temple. What makes the new universe so dazzling is not gold or jewels but rather the presence of God. The whole world is his holy of holies. The task given to Adam, to rule the world for God, has been successfully completed by Jesus Christ. The goal of all redemptive history will be obtained. "They will see his face" (22:4). They will see the King in his beauty.[15]

Amen! Even so come Lord Jesus!

Endnotes

Introduction

1. See Owen Strachen, 'Of Scholars and Saints', in Kevin J. Vanhoozer and Owen Strachen, *The Pastor as Public Theologian: Reclaiming a Lost Vision* (Baker Books, 2015), p. 80.

2. Ibid., p. 81.

3. J.I. Packer, *A Quest for Godliness: The Puritan Vision of the Christian Life* (Wheaton, IL: Crossway, 1994), p. 102.

4. Ibid., p. 103.

5. Francesca Aran Murphy, 'The Book of Revelation', in *Dictionary for Theological Interpretation of the Bible* (Baker, Academic, 2005, ed. Kevin J. Vanhoozer), p. 686.

6. Ian Paul, *Revelation*, Tyndale New Testament Commentaries, Vol. 20 (Inter Varsity Press, Academic, 2018), p. 1.

7. Kevin J. Vanhoozer, 'In the Evangelical Mood', *The Pastor as Public Theologian: Reclaiming a Lost Vision,* p. 109.

8. William Hendriksen, *More than Conquerors* (Baker Book House, 1986), p. 7.

Chapter 1

1. Os Guinness, *The Gravedigger File* (London: Hodder & Stoughton, 1983), pp. 42, 45.

2. D.A. Carson, 'Approaching the Bible', in *New Bible Commentary*, 21st Century Edition (Inter Varsity Press, 1994), p. 15.

3. See, Bruce W. Winter, *Roman Wives, Roman Widows: The Appearance of New Women and the Pauline Communities* (Grand Rapids, MI: W.B. Eerdmans, 2003).

4. In Bryan Wilson, *Religion in Secular Society: A Sociological Comment* (London: C.A. Watts, 1966), p. xiv. Peter Berger defines it as, 'The process by which sectors of society and culture are removed from the domination of religious institutions and symbols.' In other words, this is a movement of change which takes place through the structures of society, especially the spheres of science, technology, bureaucracy and the media which results in religious ideas becoming less meaningful and religious institutions more marginal.' See Melvin Tinker, 'Secularisation: Myth or Menace? An Assessment of Modern "Worldliness"', *Themelios*, Volume 38. Issue 3.

5. Os Guinness, *Dining with the Devil: The Mega Church Movement Flirts with Modernity* (Grand Rapids: Baker, 1993), p. 41.

6. Ibid. p. 49.

7. Ibid. p. 41.

8. Ibid. p. 49.

9. George Barna, *Marketing the Church* (Navpress, 1988).

10. David F. Wells, *The Courage to be Protestant: Truth-Lovers, Marketers and Emergents in the Postmodern World* (Nottingham: IVP, 2008), pp. 57–58.

11. 'As a person imagines, so will she or he perceive, understand, love, and act.' Sang Hyun Lee, *The Philosophical Theology of Jonathan Edwards* (Princeton, NJ: Princeton University Press, 2000), p. 133.

12. David. A. de Silva, *Seeing Things John's Way: The Rhetoric of the Book of Revelation* (Louisville, KY: Westminster John Knox Press, 2009), p. 198.

13. Richard Bauckham, *The Theology of the Book of Revelation* (Cambridge University Press, 1993), p. 31.

14. See Kevin J. Vanhoozer, *Pictures at a Theological Exhibition* (Inter Varsity Press, 2016), p. 36.

15. Charles Taylor, *A Secular Age* (Cambridge, MA: Belknap Press of Harvard University Press, 2007), p. 171.

16. Ibid. p. 172.

17. Kevin J. Vanhoozer, *Hearers and Doers: A Pastor's Guide to Making Disciples Through Scripture and Doctrine* (Lexham Press, 2019), pp. 8–9.

18. David. A. de Silva, *Seeing Things John's Way*, p. 98.

19. Clifford Geertz, *The Interpretation of Cultures* (New York: Basic Books, 1973), p. 122.

20. Robert H. Mounce, *The Book of Revelation*, The New International Commentary on the New Testament (Eerdmans; Revised edition, 1997), p. 133.

21. David. A. de Silva, *Seeing Things John's Way*, p. 335.

22. See, Melvin Tinker, *That Hideous Strength: How the West Was Lost: The Cancer of Cultural Marxism in the Church, the World and the Gospel of Change* (Evangelical Press, 2018).

23. Ian Paul, *Revelation,* Tyndale New Testament Commentaries, Vol. 20 (Inter Varsity Press, Academic, 2018), p. 23.

24. The name 'Jesus' occurs fourteen times within the book and 'Christ' seven times. Given the significance of the number (seven and multiples

of seven) this in itself underscores the centrality of the second person of the Trinity.

25. Brian J. Tabb, *All Things New: Revelation as Canonical Capstone* (Inter Varsity Press, Academic, 2019), p. 3.

26. 'Confronted with John's stance toward Roman imperialism and outspoken critique (evidenced in Revelation itself), a local official if not Domitian, might well have seen relegation to an island like Patmos a politic solution.' David. A. de Silva, *Seeing Things John's Way*, p. 33.

27. That the book had a wider intended readership is clear to Richard Bauckham, 'The definitiveness with which he seems to envisage his prophecy as the final culmination of the whole biblical prophetic tradition suggests a relevance for all Christian churches. This is what the number seven must indicate … seven is the number of completion.' Richard Bauckham, *The Theology of the Book of Revelation*, p. 16.

28. Ian Paul, 'What does Revelation 4 and 5 tell us about the Trinity?' www.psephizo.com/revelation/what-does-rev-4-5-tell-us-about-the-trinity/ (accessed 2021-03-16).

29. See Graeme Goldsworthy, *Gospel and Wisdom* (Paternoster, 1995), p. 161, and also the comment of Gordon Jessup, *No Strange God* (Olive Press, 1976), p. 105, 'It has been suggested by at least one notable Jewish scholar and professor, that there was a time when Judaism could have accepted a Trinitarian doctrine of God. By the time of Maimonides, Christian anti-Jewish behaviour had made this emotionally impossible. From his time onwards it has also been intellectually impossible (except by the grace of God) for an Orthodox Jew to believe in a God whose Unity is so complex that it can also be called Trinity.'. It was the twelfth century Jewish philosopher, Maimonides who introduced the use of the word *yachid*, which is related to *echad* but which emphasises the solitary nature of oneness.

30. John Calvin, *Institutes*, 1:13.2, Ed. John T. McNeill (Westminster Press, 1960).

31. Michael Jensen, 'The Very Practical Doctrine of the Trinity', in *The Briefing*, July 2000.

Chapter 2

1. See: *The Encyclopaedia of Apocalypticism*, Ed. John J. Collins (New York: Continuum, 1998).

2. P.J. Leithart, *Revelation 1–11* (T&T Clark, International Theological Commentary, 2018).

3. Brian J. Tabb, *All Things New*, p. 8.

4. David. A. de Silva, *Seeing Things John's Way*, p. 115.

5. Brian J. Tabb, *All Things New*, p. 2.

6. Ian Paul, *Revelation*, p. 4.

7. Brian J. Tabb, *All Things New*, p. 31.

8. In the Greek there is a linguistic irregularity, for [he] 'who is, and who was and who is to come' is in the nominative case rather than the expected genitive which suggests that John is using it as a fixed title.

9. Anselm, 'On the Fall of the Devil', *The Major Works* (Oxford University Press, 1998), p. 194.

10. Richard Bauckham, *The Theology of the Book of Revelation,* p. 27.

11. Brian J. Tabb, *All Things New*, p. 47.

12. See Melvin Tinker, *Intended for Good: The Providence Of God* (InterVarsity Press, 2012).

13. Richard Bauckham, *The Theology of the Book of Revelation*, p. 73.

14. Brian J. Tabb, *All Things New*, p. 56.

15. 'It is striking that the first part of this is directed to Jesus, rather than God (made clear by reference to his blood). What God has done for us in

Jesus was indeed the act of Jesus himself, and not simply an instrument of the Father's will.' Ian Paul, *Revelation,* p. 63.

16. John's use of 'seven Spirits' is distinctive and has been interpreted in two main ways: 1. Seven angels or 2. The sevenfold Holy Spirit. I take it to be the latter, not least because angels are not seen to be the source of 'grace and peace', only God. When we deal with the Spirit in more detail we shall also see that one of the primary influences on John adopting this term is Zechariah 4.

17. John Calvin, *New Testament Commentaries, Volume 10* (Eerdmans, 1964), p. 330.

18. Richard Sibbes, 'A Description of Christ' in *Works*, Volume I (Edinburgh: The Banner of Trusth Trust, 1973 reprint), p. 12.

19. Cited by Matthew Barrett, in *None Greater* (Baker Books, 2019), p. 42.

Chapter 3

1. David F. Wells, *God in the Whirlwind: How the Holy-Love of God Reorients Our World* (Wheaton, IL: Crossway, 2014), p. 108.

2. David A. de Silva, *Seeing Things John's Way*, p. 97.

3. Os Guinness, *Unspeakable — Facing up to Evil in an Age of Genocide* (Harper/Collins, 2005), pp. 56–57.

4. Beale argues that Revelation 4–5 corresponds closely to the order and structure of Daniel 7. G.K. Beale, *The Use of Daniel in Jewish Apocalyptic Literature and the Revelation of St John* (Wipf & Stock, 2010), pp. 181–182.

5. L. Thompson, *The Book of Revelation: Apocalypse and Empire* (Oxford University Press, 1990), p. 162.

6. Ian Paul, 'What Does Revelation 4–5 Tell Us About the Trinity', www. psephizo.com/revelation/what-does-rev-4-5-tell-us-about-the-trinity (accessed 2021-03-16).

7. The nature of the relation between language and our knowledge is captured by two Latin terms: *res significate* referring to the *object* in view and *modus significandi* — the *way* in which a particular term can be applied. It was the mediaeval theologian Thomas Aquinas who argued that the *res significate* does not change in any way, but the *modus significandi* can. Is God 'good' in the same way a human is? Not really. 'Because God is infinite and unified, the *modus significandi* of a term applied to God and creatures is different. We cannot possibly comprehend just how God is good, and so although we do have an understanding of goodness, there is inevitably a vagueness and inadequacy when we use the term of the perfect Being.' Katherine Rogers, *A Perfect Being Theology. Reason and Religion* (Edinburgh University Press, 2000), p. 17.

8. John's grammar also reflects the impossibility of describing God 'as he is'. The throne is described without using finite verbs, and all in the nominative case. But when John turns to things *around* the throne, he moves to the accusative case. And so if some things in heaven can be described as objects as we might describe things on earth, that does *not* apply to the throne and the one seated upon it.

9. G.K. Beale, *The Book of Revelation*, The New International Greek Testament Commentary (Grand Rapids, MI: Wm. B. Eerdmans, 2013), p. 321.

10. Ian Paul argues against this interpretation, but comes to the same conclusion presented here, that these figures represent in some way the whole people of God, Ian Paul, *Revelation,* p. 122.

11. G.K. Beale, *Revelation*, p. 322.

12. Ibid. p. 323.

13. Robert H. Mounce, *The Book of Revelation,* p. 139.

14. Josephus, *Jewish War* 7:71.

15. Richard Bauckham, *The Theology of the Book of Revelation*, p. 33.

16. David F. Wells, *God in the Whirlwind*, p. 111.

17. Sam Storms, *One Thing* (Christian Focus, 2004), pp. 70–71.

Chapter 4

1. G.K. Beale, *Revelation*, p. 340.

2. Cited in Francis Schaeffer and Koop C. Everett, *Whatever Happened to the Human Race?* (London: Marshall, Morgan and Scott, 1980), pp. 97–98.

3. Stig Björkman, *Woody Allen on Woody Allen* (New York: Grove Press, 1993).

4. Richard Bauckham, *The Theology of the Book of Revelation*, p. 74. 'The novelty of John's symbol lies in its representation of the sacrificial death of Christ as the fulfilment of Jewish hopes of the messianic conqueror.' Richard Bauckham, *The Climax of Prophecy* (Edinburgh: T&T Clark, 1996), p. 184.

5. Brian J. Tabb, *All Things New*, p. 59.

6. Thomas Schreiner, *The King in His Beauty: A Biblical Theology of the Old and New Testaments* (Baker Academic, 2013), p. 625.

7. Cited by David F. Wells in *God in the Wasteland* (W.B. Eerdmans, 1994), p. 35.

8. See Melvin Tinker, *Veiled in Flesh: The Incarnation — What It Means And Why It Matters* (Inter Varsity Press, 2019).

9. See D.A. Carson, *The Sermon on the Mount* (Grand Rapids: Baker, 1978), p. 12.

10. Richard H. Schmidt, *Glorious Companions: Five Centuries of Anglican Spirituality* (Grand Rapids, MI: W.B. Eerdmans, 2003), p. 320.

11. R.T. France, 'The Worship of Jesus', in *Christ the Lord: Studies Presented to Donald Guthrie* (Inter Varsity Press, 1982), pp. 24–25.

12. Ibid., pp. 32–33. 'It seems ... that the worship of Jesus must be understood as indicating the inclusion of Jesus in the being of one God defined by monotheistic worship.' Richard Bauckham, *The Theology of the Book of Revelation*, p. 60.

13. David A. de Silva, *Seeing Things John's Way*, p. 195.

14. Ibid., p. 196.

15. Ibid., p. 197.

16. A.W. Tozer, *The Knowledge of the Holy: The Attributes of God — Their Meaning in the Christian Life* (Harrisburg, PA: Christian Publications, 1961), p. 10.

17. This was recognised by B.F. Westcott many years ago, 'The modern conception of Christ pleading in heaven his passion, offering his blood on behalf of men, has no foundation in [the epistle to] Hebrews. His glorified humanity is the eternal pledge of the absolute efficacy of his accomplished work. He pleads by his very presence on the Father's throne.' B.F. Westcott, *The Epistle to the Hebrews* (Macmillan), p. 230.

18. James B. Torrance, *Worship, Community and the Triune God of Grace* (Downers Grove, IL: InterVarsity Press, Academic, 1996).

19. Jonathan Edwards, 'Ethical Writings', in *The Works of Jonathan Edwards* (New Haven and London: Yale University Press, 1957–2008), 8:145.

Chapter 5

1. Max Lucado, *A Gentle Thunder: Hearing God Through the Storm* (Word Publishing, 1995), p. 3.

2. John V. Taylor, *The Go-Between God* (SCM Christian Classics, 2003).

3. Ian Paul, *Revelation*, p. 62.

4. G.K. Beale *Revelation*, pp. 189–190.

5. See, Mikeal C. Parsons, 'Exegesis "By the Numbers": Numerology and the New Testament,' *Perspectives in Religious Studies,* Volume 35, Issue 1, p. 28.

6. J.L. Mangina, cited in Brian J. Tabb, *All Things New*, p. 71.

7. Brian J. Tabb, *All Things New,* p. 71.

8. John A. Studerbaker Jr. *The Lord is the Spirit: The Authority of the Holy Spirit in Contemporary Theology and Church Practice* (Eugene, OR: Pickwick Publications, 2008), pp. 125–153.

9. Ian Paul, 'Did John See Revelation as a Vision?' www.psephizo.com/revelation/did-john-see-revelation-as-a-vision (accessed 2021–03–16).

10. Ibid.

11. Cited in Michael Reeves, *Delighting in the Trinity* (Downer Grove, IL: InterVarsity Press, Academic, 2012), p. 94.

12. Cited in Michael Reeves, *Rejoicing in Christ* (Downers Grove, IL: InterVarsity, 2015), p. 11.

13. Kevin J. Vanhoozer, 'True Pictures', in *Pictures at a Theological Exhibition* (Downers Grove, IL: InterVarsity Press, Academic, 2016), p. 79.

14. Ibid., p. 79.

15. Stephen Charnock, *Existence and Attributes of God*, 1:385.

16. Ibid., 1:387.

17. Jonathan Edwards makes a similar point, 'Heaven is the palace or presence chamber of the Supreme Being who is both the cause and source of all holy love. God, indeed, with respect to his essence is everywhere. He fills heaven and earth. But yet he is said on some accounts more especially to be in some places rather than others. He was said of old to dwell in the land of Israel above all other lands, and in Jerusalem above all other cities in that land, and in the temple above all other houses in that city, and in the holy of holies above all other apartments in that temple, and on the mercy seat over the ark above all

other places in the holy of holies. But heaven is his dwelling place above all other places in the universe.' Cited in Strachan and Sweeney, *Jonathan Edwards on Heaven and Hell* (Moody Press, 2010), p. 105.

18. Kevin J. Vanhoozer, 'Praising God in Song', in *Pictures at a Theological Exhibition*, pp. 144–145.

19. R.A. Torrey, *The Person and Work of the Holy Spirit* (New York: Fleming H. Revell, 1910), p. 15.

20. Richard Bauckham, *The Theology of the Book of Revelation*, p. 73, see also, Brian J. Tabb, *All Things New*, pp. 97–101.

21. Cited in Michael Green, *The Empty Cross of Jesus* (Hodder and Stoughton, 1984), p. 203.

22. Don Cormack, *Killing Fields, Living Fields* (Monarch, 1997), p. 234.

23. Jonathan Edwards, 'Ethical Writings', in *The Works of Jonathan Edwards* (New Haven and London: Yale University Press, 1957–2008), 8:386.

Chapter 6

1. I am grateful to Peter Lewis for this observation.

2. John J. Bimson argues 'that Behemoth and Leviathan are mythical chaos monsters representing cosmic forces hostile to God and inimical to human welfare.' In 'Fierce Beasts and Free Processes: A Proposed Reading of God's Speeches in Job' in *Wisdom, Science and the Scriptures: Essays in Honour of Ernest Lucas*, Ed. Stephen Finamore and John Weaver (Pickwick Publications, Oregon, 2014), p. 18. See also Melvin Tinker: *If God is so Good Why Are Things so Bad?* (Evangelical Press, 2019), chapter 6.

3. In Isaiah 27:1 the same symbol is used to depict evil rulers who threaten God's people with captivity, as did Pharaoh of old. God promises to deliver his people from such a monstrous tyrant: 'In that day, the LORD will punish with his sword, his fierce, great and powerful sword,

Leviathan the gliding serpent, Leviathan the coiling serpent; he will slay the monster of the sea.'

4.   David A. de Silva, *Seeing Things John's Way*, p. 199.

5.   See John H. Walton, *Job*: The NIV Application Commentary (Zondervan, 2013) p. 64 (*hassatan* — challenger).

6.   Erwin Lutzer, *The Serpent of Paradise: The Incredible Story of How Satan's Rebellion Serves God's Purposes* (Moody, 1998).

7.   In part, this is the significance of God demonstrating his control over the Red *Sea* when Israel was being pursued by Pharaoh's armies, 'God conquers Pharaoh's armies with the forces of chaos that God had already conquered (as it were) at creation. This must have seemed the sweetest of victories in the eyes of Israel: their God, the Lord God, displayed his absolute sovereignty not only over Pharaoh but also over all the gods and symbols of chaos in the ancient Near East. There is cosmic significance in the waters of the Red Sea.' Vanhoozer, 'Moses' Magnificat' in, *Pictures at a Theological Exhibition*, p. 150.

8.   Thomas R. Schreiner, *The King in His Beauty: A Biblical Theology of the Old and New Testaments* (Baker Academic, 2013), p. 618.

9.   Greg Carey, *Elusive Apocalypse: Reading Authority in the Revelation to John,* Studies in American Biblical Hermeneutics 15 (Macon, GA: Mercer University Press, 1999).

10. David de Silva, *Seeing Things John's Way*, p. 198.

11. Cited in Os Guinness, *Unspeakable* (HarperCollins, 2005) pp. 182–184.

12. See Melvin Tinker, *That Hideous Strength: How the West was Lost — The Cancer of Cultural Marxism* (Evangelical Press, 2018).

13. Cited by Gavin Ashenden, 'Sinister agenda to replace families with Big Brother', ashenden.org/2018/03/15/when-the-silly-becomes-the-sinister-the-latest-round-in-the-culture-wars (accessed 2021-03-16).

14. www.thetimes.co.uk/article/it-s-wrong-to-protest-about-the-teaching-of-gay-relationships-tog85vxx6 (accessed 2021-03-16).

15. https://anglicanmainstream.org/the-war-on-children-the-comprehensive-sexuality-education-agenda/ (accessed 2021-03-29).

16. See Melvin Tinker, *That Hideous Strength: How The West was Lost* pp. 81–85.

17. See Mikeal C. Parsons, 'Exegesis "By the Numbers": Numerology and the New Testament,' 4; François Bovon, "Names and Numbers in Early Christianity," *NTS* 47 (2001), 267; Adela Yarbro Collins, 'Numerical Symbolism in Jewish and Early Christian Apocalyptic Literature,' ANRW 2.21.2:1221–87.

18. See Ian Paul, *Revelation*, p. 239.

19. Ibid., p. 240.

20. Thomas Schreiner, *The King in his Beauty*, p. 620.

21. 'One of the fundamental themes of Revelation, therefore, is that believers must endure persecution in order to receive the final reward of the kingdom. If they capitulate and worship the beast, they will face the same judgement as the beast, the false prophet and Satan and suffer torment for ever (14:9–11. Churches are commended for their endurance and persistence (2:2,3,19; 3:10) and John summons them to endure to the end and keep Jesus' commands (13:10; 14:12). Jesus functions as an example for believers because he was "the faithful witness" in his suffering (1:5), and believers, like Jesus, must be faithful even in the midst of opposition and in the face of death.' Ibid., pp. 619–620.

22. Karl Olsen, *Passion* (Harper and Row Publishers, 1963), pp. 116–117.

Chapter 7

1. Os Guinness, *Time for Truth* (InterVarsity Press, 2000) p. 9.

2. Richard Bauckham, *The Theology of the Book of Revelation*, p. 104.

3. Ibid. p. 105.

4. Michael Green, *The Empty Cross of Jesus*, pp. 208–209.

5. Richard Bauckham, *The Theology of the Book of Revelation,* p. 105.

6. Cited by John Piper, *Future Grace*, pp. 263–4.

7. Robert Royalty, *The Streets of Heaven: The Ideology of Wealth in the Apocalypse of John* (Macon, GA: Mercer University Press, 1998), p. 33.

8. D.H. Lawrence, *The Apocalypse of John* (New York: A.A. Knopf, 1931), p. 117.

9. D.A. Carson, *The God Who is There* (Baker Books, 2010), p. 208.

10. David A. de Silva, *Seeing Things John's Way*, p. 173.

Chapter 8

1. C.S. Lewis, *The Last Battle, The Chronicles of Narnia* (New York: Harper Collins, 1994), p. 73.

2. Brian J. Tabb, *All Things New,* p. 201.

3. John Piper, *God is the Gospel* (Crossway Books, 2005), pp. 151–152.

4. Cited in Strachan and Owen, *Jonathan Edwards on Heaven and Hell,* p. 93.

5. 'John's portrayal of the entire new creation as a city, a temple, and a garden is exactly what the OT in various places anticipated.' Greg Beale, *The Temple and the Church's Mission: A Biblical Theology of the Dwelling Place of God* (Downers Grove, IL: InterVarsity, 2004), p. 759.

6. 'The critical question for our generation — and for every generation — is this: If you could have heaven, with no sickness, and with all your friends you ever had on earth, and all the food you had ever liked, and all the leisure activities you ever enjoyed, and all the natural beauties you ever saw, all the physical pleasures you ever tasted, and no human

conflict or any natural disasters, could you be satisfied with heaven if Christ were not there?' John Piper, *God is the Gospel*, p. 15.

7.   George Bernard Shaw, 'The Horror of the Perpetual Holiday,' in *The Works of Bernard Shaw*, Vol. 13 (Constable, 1930), p. 35.

8.   Cited by Stephen Travis, *I Believe in the Second Coming of Jesus* (Grand Rapids, MI: W.B. Eerdmans, 1982), p. 176.

9.   J.A. Conyers, *The Eclipse of Heaven: Rediscovering the Hope of a World Beyond* (Downers Grove, IL, 1992), p. 11.

10. J.C. Ryle, in *Holiness: Its Nature: Its Hindrances, Difficulties, and Roots* (1877; repr., Charles Nolan, 2001), p. 384.

11. Kevin J. Vanhoozer, *Hearers and Doers: A Pastor's Guide to Making Disciples Through Scripture and Doctrine* (Lexham Press, 2019), p. 143.

12. Cited in Strachan and Sweeney, *Jonathan Edwards on Heaven and Hell*, p. 95.

13. Michael Reeves, *Delighting in the Trinity*, p. 123.

14. Cited in John Piper, *God is the Gospel*, p. 145.

15. Thomas R. Schreiner, *The King in His Beauty: A Biblical Theology of the Old and New Testaments* (Baker Academic, 2013), p. 629.